Family Development I

Understanding Us

Family Development I

Understanding Us

by
Patrick J. Carnes

Series Editor: Daniel B. Wackman

ISBN 0917340-10-8
First Printing, January, 1981

Illustrations: Barry Ives
Book Design and Graphics: Robert Friederichsen
Printing: Printing Arts, Inc.

INTERPERSONAL
COMMUNICATION PROGRAMS, INC.
300 Clifton Avenue
Minneapolis, Minnesota 55403
(612) 871-7388

PREFACE

The family is under increasing pressure. Most families experience the pressure in a number of ways. Sometimes it is just having less time together or it is having difficulty in getting things done. Other times it is the more difficult task of understanding another person in the family with whom you are at odds. Perhaps one of the most difficult is a family adjusting to change especially as children and parents mature. None is more difficult than a basic issue in the family which does not ever become resolved even though everything else is going well.

UNDERSTANDING US was written to assist members of a family in better understanding themselves as they struggle with the challenges of the late twentieth century. It is not intended as a solution for severely troubled families, although they will benefit as well. It is the first in a series of programs which are designed to make sound concepts and experiences available for all families who want them.

UNDERSTANDING US is a wellness book for families. It is an invitation for family members to explore together the fundamental bonds which hold them together. If your experience is similar to that of other UNDERSTANDING US families, you may also find new options as a family. The most important goal is to recognize, appreciate, and enhance those many strengths you already have together.

ORIGINS OF UNDERSTANDING US

Ten years ago a group of church staff members invited a large number of families to join us in the parish gymnasium to explore family relationships. The results were so successful we had to repeat the initial program many times over that year. We knew that could only happen if we were meeting a genuine need of families. As a staff member and teacher, I became aware that it was the most exciting work I had ever done.

In 1972 I and a number of colleagues—principally Mary Pat Brygger, Herb Laube and Chester Meyers—launched a project called **Becoming Us.** Funded by the United Church of Christ, it was an ecumenical effort to make family-focused education available on a much broader level. A major part of its success as a project was that it further demonstrated that the need for families to learn together was widespread and extended to rural as well as urban families. **Becoming Us** also showed that a viable curriculum could be taught to the families themselves so that they might teach others.

In 1976 I became the Director of the Family Renewal Center at Fairview Southdale Hospital. Our initial role was to be a treatment center for chemically dependent families, a role which has since expanded considerably. One of my functions was to continue the development of curriculum experience for families. Because my attention was almost exclusively on the therapeutic families, I was even more struck by the regenerative powers released by families learning together.

It was Sherod Miller and Dan Wackman of Interpersonal Communication Programs, Inc., who invited me to develop UNDERSTANDING US. Their encouragement and their knowledge in the field of family and marriage enrichment were enormous resources in the development of this program. Also, Professor David Olson of the University of Minnesota's Family Social Science Department provided special impetus with his "circumplex" model of family systems. Called the Family Map in UNDERSTANDING US, it is key to the conceptual organization of the program.

Currently, there are almost one thousand instructors throughout the United States who have been trained to teach UNDERSTANDING US. Their reports have been invaluable in preparing the manuscript for this book. Their success also shows that families do wish to learn together. In an age in which education is conducted assembly-line fashion, first grade through college, UNDERSTANDING US does offer a learning experience in which people can be all ages and still learn from one another. These instructors can give testimony to what clinicians and therapists have known for decades—that families learn best about themselves together not separately.

ABOUT THE AUTHOR

Patrick J. Carnes is the Director of the Family Renewal Center of Fairview Southdale Hospital in Edina, Minnesota. He is married and has four children. His Ph.D. is in teaching and supervision of counselors and counselor education, family education and counseling' and organizational development from the University of Minnesota. He also lectures widely and is a consultant to academic, medical, social service and criminal justice organizations.

ACKNOWLEDGEMENTS

It is a long way from those crowded nights in the parish gymnasium. In that sense, UNDERSTANDING US incorporates over ten years of experience. It also reflects the contributions of many beyond those already acknowledged including:

— The staff of the Family Learning Center of Saint Mary of the Lake Church where it all started, Father Anthony Louis, Tom Sweeney, Frances Meyers, and George Meullner.

— The management and staff of the Family Renewal Center at Fairview Southdale Hospital where it continues, including Al Nohre, Ellie Killorin, Jerry Larsen, Glenice Anderson and Ann Golla. Special appreciation is exteneded to Miriam Ingelbritson and Dave Walsh of the Family Renewal Center who, in their roles as Instructor Training Associates, made substantial contributions to the program and its curriculum.

— My family, including my parents, my wife, Terri, and my children, David, Stefanie, Jennifer, and Erin. It is their stories I have often shared and their support and patience that was indispensible. To them this book is dedicated.

CONTENTS

PREFACE
    Origins Of UNDERSTANDING US
    About The Author
    Acknowledgements

INTRODUCTION 11
    Some Basics About Families 13
    Outline of UNDERSTANDING US 16
    How To Use The Book 17
    Joining An UNDERSTANDING US Group 21

1. ADAPTING 25
    Family Adaptability 26
    To Be Structured Or Flexible 30
    Too Structured Or Too Flexible 31
    Responsible Parental Discipline And Leadership 39
    Suggestions To Parents About Your Family Adaptability 44
    Exercises For Chapter 1 49

2. CARING..63
    Family Cohesion...64
    To Be Connected Or Separated..............................68
    Too Connected Or Too Separated............................70
    Responsible Parental Care Giving..........................77
    Suggestions To Parents About Your Family Cohesion.........80
    The Blending Of Two Epics.................................84
    Exercises For Chapter 2...................................93

3. GROWING...107
    The Family Map..108
    The Area Of Family Wellness—Regions I And II..............109
    Region II...111
    Region III..112
    Exploring The Family Map..................................115
    The Identity Cycle..121
    The Four Phases Of Individual Development.................121
    The Search For Identity...................................127
    Childhood And The Identity Cycle..........................129
    Adolescence And The Identity Cycle........................132
    Adulthood And The Identity Cycle..........................136
    Self-Concept Development And The Identity Cycle...........141
    Exercises For Chapter 3...................................144

4. CHANGING..157
    Family And Identity.......................................161
    Identity Cycles And The Family Comfort Zone...............167
    Unbalanced Family Systems.................................170
    The Family Life Cycle—Stability And Change................175
    Family Growth Patterns....................................176
    Blocks To Change..180
    Family Wellness...187
    Exercises For Chapter 4...................................191

APPENDIX..201
    Couple Communication I....................................201
    Working Together..202

INTRODUCTION

One blustery afternoon in early March, I went to pick up my daughter, Jennifer, at her Montessori school. Out on the snow-covered playground, her friends were totally engrossed. in being "Cookie Monsters." Having had a very trying day, the prospect of crawling around and playing surly looked like a good cure for my bad mood. On my hands and knees I started across the playground doing my very best "Cookie Monster" act. Soon I was pinned in a snowbank by a crowd of snow-suited five year olds. I answered their fierce growls just as fiercely until we were all convulsed with the giggles.

Picking myself up, I told Jennifer we had to go. She responded by saying, "Dad, I have to show you something first." Instantly, those earlier feelings of frustration and impatience returned. I said, "No, Jennifer. We have to go **now**!" I emphasized "now" in a tone which meant I would not tolerate delay. Jennifer's answer was equally determined, "Dad, this is **important**!" The even look of the eye and the resolute stance, complete with the hand on the hip, were so reminiscent of her mother when she was determined that I had to smile.

Jennifer promptly wheeled and led me to a corner of the school. Tucked between the red brick wall of the school and a snowbank stood a solitary clover. It had to be the first harbinger of spring and was truly an astounding find. More importantly, looking at the pale green shoot, I was filled with the awareness of how preoccupied I was about the day's events. There were other things more significant including playing "Cookie Monster" in

the snow and discovering a courageous clover. The most significant was the realization of the great gift my child had given me—the gift of perspective about the importance of work.

This event parallels what UNDERSTANDING US is all about. It is about parents setting limits for their children and how that affects their values and sense of self. It is also about adults learning from their children and making commitments in their own lifestyle. UNDERSTANDING US approaches families as the foundation of both child and adult development.

Families are human systems in which people grow. UNDERSTAND-ING US is designed to help family members understand themselves as a growth system. Like any system, a family needs to be flexible enough to survive both the challenge of cultural change and the growth of family members. It also has to have firm boundaries upon which family members depend for constancy, support, and identity. In an era in which "throw-away" marriages co-exist with profound searches for family "roots," there is a need for a guide to the ecology of human relationships.

There are excellent books on parenting and improving relationships. They reflect, as well, our unremitting search for "the method" to raise our children or to enhance our marriage. Parenting, for example, becomes something you do to others and not a reciprocal relationship in which the adult grows. Our purpose is different. By understanding their own process, family members can reclaim their own rights as experts about whom and how they wish to become. This is not a method book. Rather it is a way for a family to explore their options together.

UNDERSTANDING US seeks to extend our awareness beyond ourselves to the intimate ecology of relationships which sustain us. The principles described are research-based and reflect current knowledge about family and marital systems. They apply to all types of families including single-parent families and blended families. The book is designed for families whose issues are common to all of us. All that is necessary is a willingness to get involved together in reading and talking over this book.

SOME BASICS ABOUT FAMILIES

The UNDERSTANDING US program recognizes some basic realities about being in a family. The first is that despite a popular image of the family as the pillar of stability, the family is constantly changing. Any parent who experiences sadness at watching a child grow too fast or who notices the aging of his/her own parents can attest that few things remain the same for long in a family.

There are two types of growth occuring simultaneously within the family. The first is the quest of each individual family member for his/her own identity. A self-concept is healthy when a person is growing and expanding in awareness and ability. It is a process which continues until death. UNDERSTANDING US is written with the conviction that the growth of adults is as important as that of their children. In fact, to grow all family members need each other. Their interdependency is the key factor of the second type of development, the growth of the family.

A family, too, is on a quest for identity. Instead of a self-concept, a family has an "Us" concept—hence the title of UNDERSTANDING US. The optimum condition for both the "Us" and the individual to grow is when a balance is achieved in the needs of each. Describing that process is the central goal of UNDERSTANDING US.

Because growth is not perfectly matched even in the most balanced of families, members develop issues with one another. Usually these issues are rooted in three basic questions every family faces simply by being a family:

1. How adaptable or flexible will we be as a family?
2. How close and involved will we be as a family?
3. How much can we depend upon and trust one another as a family?

The answers to these questions will vary considerably as a family lives over time. The family with three children under the age of six will answer the questions quite differently from the same family when all three are over twenty.

The inevitable issues, however, are not always easy to resolve. When an issue continues to be a difficulty it becomes a problem for the family affecting everyone. Usually it is due to a failure of understanding or an inability to acknowledge some essential change. UNDERSTANDING US provides ways for every family to seek new understandings of differences and to develop a new appreciation of one another:

— by learning together how a family is formed and maintained,
— by providing perspective as to how conflict occurs,
— by comparing each other's experience in the family,
— by exploring options to self-defeating cycles in the family,
— by appreciating the paradoxes contained in human relationships,
— by providing a structure for reclaiming personal responsibility in family issues,
— by developing a heightened sense of your "Us" as a family.

UNDERSTANDING US is a common learning venture in which a family can discover that through making responsible choices each member can feel good about him/herself as a separate person and as a family.

In many ways UNDERSTANDING US is an invitation to sit down and talk to one another, sort of a stock-taking time. Many families have reported that one of the most important parts of the program was the realization of how little they talked as a family. Often the talking was about things people already knew but simply had not shared with each other.

OUTLINE OF UNDERSTANDING US

UNDERSTANDING US is divided into four chapters: Adapting, Caring, Growing, and Changing. Each chapter develops a major theme. Later chapters build upon concepts established in the preceding ones. Together they form a comprehensive model of family functioning.

"Adapting," the first chapter, describes how a family adapts its own structure to meet the changing needs of family members. Variations in the degree of adaptability or flexibility among families are explored. The key factors considered include how a family gets organized, survives a crisis, and develops a value system.

"Caring" underlines the importance of cohesion and intimacy as a family. Again variations among families in levels of cohesiveness are examined with special considerations given to such factors as autonomy, permission to make mistakes, and self-concept. Having established basic principles around adaptability and cohesion, the second section of this chapter explores the central process of how a family is formed, i.e., how two family "epics" are blended to form a new family.

Chapter Three, "Growing," takes the elements of adaptability and cohesion and makes them into a Family Map™. On the Map, the blending of the epics as well as the continuing growth of the family can be plotted. The second half of the chapter introduces the next major concept of the program, the Identity Cycle. By understanding the four phases of identity—dependency, counter-dependency, independence and interdependence—each family member can assess more fully his/her role in the family environment.

"Changing," the final chapter, analyzes the basic tension between being an individual and being a family member. By understanding the Comfort Zone of their family, family members can approach issues in terms of different options as opposed to blame and ridicule.

HOW TO USE THE BOOK

Usually, this book will be used in a four-session course taught by a trained instructor. If your family is taking the course, your instructor will supply guidelines for the use of the book. The book may also be used by families who wish to read it together and by individuals who simply want to have a broader understanding of family functioning. For the latter two situations, a number of suggestions are appropriate.

Special margins have been left for you to record your reactions and questions. If other members of your family are reading it with you, they can respond to your marginal comments. The result can be a family dialogue in the book as the text challenges you to think about your lives together. This family "document" can be reviewed as the years pass to see how things have changed.

USING THE EXERCISES

One night after the final session of an UNDERSTANDING US group, a short, dapper, middle-aged man approached me and said, "Thanks for the Map." He went on to describe how he and his wife had struggled for years over whose way was right, his or hers. Now with teenagers, the conflict had extended to include them as well. He said, "What I realized was that it was like those experiments in which different people who see the same event, like a car accident, come up with different versions. It is a question of perspective." What was most important for him was that it was the first time in quite awhile that all four of them had had different opinions, and there was no bickering. In fact, he was beginning to see how others came to believe what they did.

As he told his story, his wife and teenagers came to stand by him. I was struck by how easy it was for good people who loved each other very much to end up far apart simply by defending a viewpoint. The youngest daughter said it succinctly, "We've wasted a lot of time."

UNDERSTANDING US contains many exercises which will ask family members to reflect on their family. As in this family, different people are likely to see things differently. The most successful way to use the exercises to learn more about your family is to allow each other differences of perception. You don't have to prove your own perceptions are correct. You do have to listen to others if you want to learn their perspectives about your family.

The exercises are designed to illustrate key points in each chapter and to supplement the UNDERSTANDING US program. You may not wish to do them all, or you may have time to do only one or two during the period between group sessions. However, your reading will be maximized if you do as many as possible.

Exercises ask you to do a number of different things. Some have you reflect on your family, either by yourself or together with other family members. Others involve story telling by family members. Still others have you doing things together as a family. The exercises can help you gain new insights about your family and new appreciation of your uniqueness. But also one of the main purposes of the exercises is to provide enjoyment for your family. As you do various exercises, enjoy yourselves.

The exercises are labeled to indicate who is to use them. GROUP exercises are used during sessions of an UNDERSTANDING US group. Other exercises are done between group sessions, and they are optional. FAMILY exercises are designed for use by the family as a whole. Sometimes these exercises

are preceded by activities completed by one or two family members, such as parents or children. These exercises are labeled like this: PARENT/FAMILY and CHILDREN/FAMILY. Some PARENT exercises are designed for parents only, and other CHILDREN exercises are specifically made for children. Lastly, a number of exercises can be completed alone by any member of the family; these are labeled INDIVIDUAL. Sometimes only limited space is provided in the exercise; so, if several of you do an exercise, you may need to use other paper.

Among the exercises at the end of each chapter are short exercises called Family Journal Entries. They contain questions designed to provoke thinking as a family. The format allows for family members to leave comments for one another as another way of sharing. Some people have taken the questions as starting points for writing in their personal journals. Using your personal journal is an excellent addition to the program format.

UNDERSTANDING US touches on some of the most important issues of our lives. It is not recommended as a book to read in one sitting. Each chapter takes only about a half hour to read but requires some thinking time in addition. It is best to wait a few days between chapters to allow for some reflection time. If the book is to be used on a weekend retreat, it is still best to prepare by reading only a section at a time.

JOINING AN UNDERSTANDING US GROUP

Your family can enhance your life together by enrolling in an UNDERSTANDING US course. A UU course normally is offered over a four-week period, meeting two hours each week. Ten to twelve families typically enroll. Courses are led by certified instructors.

Courses are offered in churches and synagogues, colleges and universities, adult education centers, hospital community-health programs and other organizations interested in promoting family wellness. If you do not know a certified UNDERSTANDING US instructor in your community and would like to participate in a UU course, write or call:

> Interpersonal Communication Programs, Inc.
> 300 Clifton Avenue
> Minneapolis, Minnesota 55403
> (612) 871-7388

You will be sent the names of certified instructors in your area. A form is provided on the last page of this book for that purpose.

Now, let's move to Chapter One and the first area of family development we will explore together, Adapting.

ADAPTING

CHAPTER ONE

ADAPTING

The scene takes place on a Thursday night in late August. The family is sitting down to dinner. Sue, the fifteen year old, has a delicate piece of negotiation to do. She has received an invitation to spend a weekend with a friend and attend a party which was described as the last fling for everybody before school. She wants to go badly. The problem is that this is the last weekend the family can be together at the lake. The family had learned that there were too many activities to try to be together as a family at the lake after school starts. So everyone made an agreement to keep last weekends of the summer as family weekends. This agreement is very important to Dad who places a high priority on the family being together.

Dad's immediate response is "no." Mom dutifully supports Dad's position, but also gives her daughter supportive looks since she senses the issue's importance for Sue. Mom also wants Sue to learn how to stand up for herself. As the discussion becomes more heated, Sue accuses her Dad of not really caring about her needs. Dad feels hurt and misunderstood but responds with anger. He insists that Sue honor the agreement she has made. Everyone goes to bed unhappy and with a vague premonition the weekend will not be pleasant.

Neither Dad nor Sue has unreasonable wants. Sue's investment in her peer group is natural and part of her quest for independence. Dad's desire to have the family together is also appropriate and vital to family solidarity. So the real issues are how to resolve the differences and how adaptable the family is. Every family has such issues. How does a healthy family respond to them?

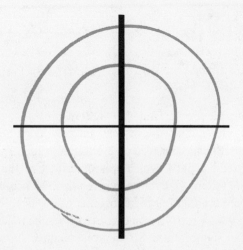

FAMILY ADAPTABILITY

Two qualities necessary for a healthy family are the capacity to plan and the capacity to work out differences when they occur. This is called adaptability. Families vary in their adaptability according to their heritage, their experience, and the developmental stages of the members. When children are small, they require an environment which is more **structured.** As children mature, parents entrust them with more responsibility and independence. The family environment then becomes more **flexible.** What is required of a parent in a structured environment is quite different from the more flexible setting.

There are five dimensions which are basic to a family's adaptability. They are leadership, discipline, negotiation, organization and values. Each of these is an important factor in how flexible or structured a family is.

LEADERSHIP

Leadership is how goals and direction are determined for the family. In a more structured family, leadership is quite stable and restricted to a few people, usually the parents. In some larger families, older children also assume leadership responsibilities. Structured families are characterized by a high degree of planning. While efforts are made to take into account every member, there are only limited options for spontaneity. Large families or families with small children are more often in this category.

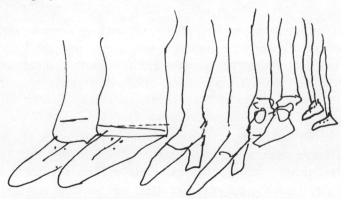

More flexible families are more democratic. All members have input, and coordination responsibilities are more likely to be shared or rotated in achieving tasks. Flexible families do develop plans, but they change plans readily and are more free to be spontaneous. Since greater flexibility demands that family members have achieved a high degree of independence, a more flexible family usually is one with somewhat older children or adolescents.

DISCIPLINE

Discipline is how parents set limits for their children. In more structured families, the limits are quite predictable. Parents have clearly established rules to cover most situations. These rules are quite explicit and do not need a lot of interpretation. The parents are responsible for the limits, believe in them personally, and enforce them. Parents match limits according to the maturity of the child.

More flexible families are not as specific in their limits. Parents focus more on situations and use general principles to assess consequences. Parents are still responsible for the limits since children know the general principles that parents will use and are certain parents will stand firmly behind them.

NEGOTIATION

In planning and problem solving, family negotiations are necessary. In more structured families, negotiations are clearly focused. Responsibilities and commitments are carefully established with minimal discussion. While selective in its options, the family is very dependable and secure—especially families with young children. Problem solving is efficient because of its emphasis on reliability.

More flexible families have relatively open negotiations and easily restructure arrangements as new options appear. This pattern is more functional where the premium is on independence, such as in a family with teenagers and where there is trust that others will carry out agreements. Problem solving is efficient because it creates solutions through the use of varied options.

ORGANIZATION

Family environments have different degrees of stability. In more structured families, the emphasis is on being sufficiently organized to prevent problems. It is a more protected environment, especially for children. A more flexible family handles routine matters with less structure and organization. Family members respond to problems as they arise.

Critical to the adaptability of the family environment is how well the family handles crises. The more flexible family usually recovers quickly from a crisis, and issues are soon resolved. The more structured family can also weather a crisis well, but it usually requires some adjustment to the routine.

VALUES

Central to a family's adaptability is its own hierarchy of values. As a person's values are central to his/her own personality, a family's sense of identity—it's Us—is based on a common set of values. Around this core of values, which is passed from generation to generation, families can again be quite structured or flexible. Relatively strict adherance to family values is one way a structured family preserves its stability. The result is a heightened sense of family solidarity which is especially important when children are young or if the family lives under threatening circumstances.

More flexible families are intent on preserving what they value too. They are also interested, however, in understanding the diversity of the world. Thus, they are more likely than structured families to incorporate new values into the family value system. The flexible family would also support more independent thinking, as might be required with a house full of teenagers.

TO BE STRUCTURED OR FLEXIBLE

All five dimensions involve common themes. More structured families tend to be relatively centralized and organized. More flexible families tend toward greater collaboration and responsiveness to changing circumstances. Structure and flexibility are both good, depending on how the family is composed and the needs of its members.

Families with younger children often find it useful to maintain a relatively structured environment. This is because young children need more predictability and more direct guidance. Families with older children, e.g., all teenagers, typically find a relatively flexible environment more comfortable because the greater freedom it allows fits better with adolescents' needs for independence.

The appropriate level of family adaptability does not just depend on the age of the children, however. Adults, too, have needs which should be taken into account. Take a family with two teenage children: normally a relatively flexible family environment would work well for them. But if the father is at an important junction in his career, with heavy demands from his job, a relatively structured environment may be ideal for him. If the mother is working outside the home, or is heavily involved in church or community activities, a more structured environment may be best for her too.

Families are quite varied, however, so only its members know if their family is sufficiently adaptable. A household of three adults, one of whom is an invalid, may be very structured. Another family with teenage children and a bonus-package toddler might involve both structured and flexible characteristics. Furthermore, since conditions are always changing, a family's adaptability is also likely to change. In any case, a family's adaptability is usually appropriate for its particular situation—until an issue emerges in which the family is too structured or too flexible.

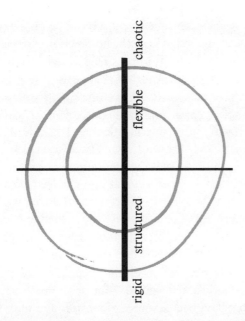

chaotic

flexible

structured

rigid

TOO STRUCTURED OR TOO FLEXIBLE

Most of us, sooner or later, do something in excess. So can families. When it happens in families, it usually becomes an issue between two or more people. Consider a family with three teenagers which is flexible about most things. The one exception is church attendance. The parents have become so insistent upon regular church attendance that their offspring are becoming resentful about church. Until it became an issue, the children enjoyed church. By not allowing exceptions, the parents were getting a result opposite of what they wanted.

Families experience difficulties with too much structure when circumstances begin to change. For example, if parents are unwilling to relax rules as children mature, they may find themselves with limits which are no longer appropriate. Another example is the family who has worked out an elaborate plan for household chores. However, it only works during the school year. Insisting on staying with it during the summer, just because it is the plan, is self-defeating.

Issues around too much flexibility often involve lack of follow-through on agreements. Signs of too much flexibility are when a family cannot arrive anywhere on time or eat a dinner with everyone there. A family which has all agreed to keep the house clean but has no one doing it has a problem with follow-through. They simply are too flexible.

Sometimes issues are not issues. What appears at first as an issue may only be a question of perspective. By reframing the situation, one might see it as a challenge or opportunity as opposed to a difficulty. Recently, I complained to my father about distractions I had while working. He shared with me an incident out of my teenage years. He used to harass me about studying with the radio on. His argument was that I would not be able to concentrate. I responded that music helped me to study better. As he reflected on it, he came to the conclusion that I was right. Life is full of interruptions and distractions. He too needed to learn how to concentrate in the midst of the distraction to get his work done. Sometimes an issue is solved by looking at it in a different way.

No amount of perspective can resolve some issues. Solutions have to be negotiated and adjustments made. Almost all families have had some specific issues that have been a source of tension. For most families these issues remain situational and are resolved in time. However, some families have so many unresolvable issues that the family environment itself becomes a problem. This happens when a family passes from being too flexible into **chaos** or, at the other end, when a family passes from being too structured into **rigidity.**

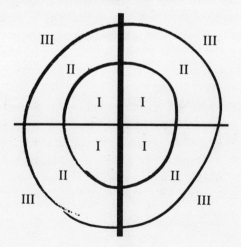

Region I
Well-functioning families

Region II
Families with issues

Region III
Families with problems

UNDER-RESPONSIBLE LIMITS—
THE CHAOTIC ENVIRONMENT

   Some families are characterized by under-responsible parenting. Rules
are seldom enforced and always changing. The family enviornment is
chaotic, as opposed to flexible or structured. In this case, parents relin-
quish personal responsibility for limit setting and rely on external controls such as church, school, and social institutions to limit behavior.

Adding to the chaos is that promises and commitments are not kept. Family members cannot **depend upon** others to do what they say they will. Since the family is the place where most of our dependency needs are met consistently, chaos in a family is serious.

Fundamental to the chaotic family environment is a chaotic marriage. The couple in this family has never really developed a contract with one another. Instead they endlessly negotiate, but nothing ever gets resolved or pinned down. Basically one or both marriage partners fails to take a stand and stick with it. With neither adult taking a stand, the family has no leader. The rules in the family are seldom agreed upon explicitly and, when they are enforced, it is done arbitrarily.

With the parents setting the tone, it is hard to assess responsibility in a chaotic family. There are so many issues left outstanding that, as soon as a family member starts to be held accountable, s/he can dredge up so many other unsettled matters that the issue quickly becomes clouded again. Even simple duties, like household chores, are subject to dramatic changes in terms of who is to do them and how they are to be done.

One of the signs of a chaotic family's under-responsibility is that they do not plan together for the future. They drift from crisis to crisis with an ever-present sense of unpreparedness. Just as a person feels good at having achieved success, families also have a sense of pride about themselves when they accomplish something together. Instead of pride, however, the chaotic family often feels disappointed at their inability to organize and accomplish.

An inability to plan as a family is partially rooted in not having a core of values as a family. A coherent set of values is necessary to prioritize and sustain a family's effort. Starting with the parents, a chaotic family does not share a common set of values. The result may be reliance on external standards such as the government, school or church instead of parents taking personal responsibility for specific standards.

All families have their periods of chaos. Stressful life events, such as moving, natural disasters and job changes, can create the unexpected. Or maybe a family just goes through a period of letting things go for awhile. For the family where chaos is a consistent lifestyle, however, the consequences may be serious.

For example, research indicates that the chaos which often surrounds abusive drinking has a great impact on children. A given set of rules will prevail until the parents start fighting, which may result in harsh interpretation of the rules for the children. Then, when the fighting has evolved into a drinking bout, the rules for the children again change, survival being the main one. Finally, during the period of hangover, shameful parents are extremely indulgent, creating yet a third set of rules.

The results are that children in chaotic alcoholic families cannot count on the family structure remaining the same at a time when they need consistency. Thus, they may begin a life-long search for something they can count on, often alcohol or drugs. Children who live with chemically-dependent parents are three times more likely to become dependent themselves. Thus, the cycle repeats itself.

While there are many different outcomes from living in a chaotic environment, there is one common element. Family members end up as persons without a core, searching for a structure, an organization, or a drug to give them a sense of identity. Often, they become under-responsible people, just as their parents were, an under-responsibility based on a distrust of their own efforts at self-determination. Frequently the distrust is reinforced by repeated disappointments.

OVER-RESPONSIBLE LIMITS—THE RIGID ENVIRONMENT

The other extreme of family environment, the rigid family, suffers from over-responsible parenting. The belief in this family is that people will not act responsibly without a high degree of control and structure. In the chaotic family, members distrust themselves. In the rigid family, the distrust is of others. The result in the rigid family is an elaborate effort to assure that all members behave properly. Parental standards are inflexible. There are also many rules reflecting the parental effort to control all outcomes. Parents insist on enforcing rules to the letter because they believe this builds character and responsibility. They also believe that children cannot be trusted to behave responsibly without a heavy rule structure.

Parents in rigid families overestimate their ability to control all the influences on their offspring. By not selecting the major areas of importance and focusing on these areas, parental energies become diffused into struggles with their children over issues of minimal significance. Resistance is perceived as disrespect which requires increased pressure. The unrelenting rigidity creates struggles which increase with the child's age.

The marriage contract in the rigid family is often missing a negotiation clause. The result is that there is little information flow between spouses and great resistance to doing things in a new way. Decisions are based on rigid stereotypes with very little tolerance for ambiguity. Real differences which could be profitably discussed are sacrificed in the interest of promoting family solidarity and avoiding conflict. The couple is closed to options, and their relationship becomes brittle.

Leadership in a rigid family supplies powerful direction but severely limits important information and suggestions upon which to make decisions. Combined with minimal negotiation, a rigid leadership style does not foster decision-making skills in other family members.

Organizationally, the family meets common goals, but at a high price. At the least, there is a risk of restricting the fun and spontaneity of being together. At the worst, the family "bureaucracy" might become so burdensome as to be totally unable to respond to the changing needs of family members. A real crisis might throw the whole system off balance.

In the rigid family, values are identified with so strongly that there often exists a distrust of people who do not share the same values. The most disabling part of a rigid value structure is that, when the family cannot adapt in the light of new information, reality is sacrificed in order to hold on to a cherished value.

Rigid families suffer most stress when there is a prospect of change. They are closed systems in which the new or the different are suspect. This is why adolescence is so traumatic in a rigid family. Requests for greater independence are minimally acknowledged rather than supported. Parents tend to view kids as "not measuring up" or as immature. Children feel distrusted and confined. They can respond by complying to parental pressure and meeting the family standards, but this response runs the risk of failing to establish their own identity. Or, alternatively, they may respond by seeking extremes in defiance of the family's inflexibility. At a mild level this may take the form of dress, music and peers.

In severe cases it may mean pursuing a career or joining a movement, cause, or a religion antithetical to parental dictates.

Rigid families, like chaotic families, impact on the self-concepts of family members. Rules can come to be perceived as a personal threat because compliance may mean the loss of personal identity. Out of this can grow a distrust of others so that, for example, as adults they may have difficulty working in structures which demand personal accountability. As in chaotic families, the ultimate issue for members of rigid families is establishing "who I am."

RESPONSIBLE PARENTAL DISCIPLINE AND LEADERSHIP

All family members have an impact on a family's adaptability. However, parents have a special impact because, through their leadership and disciplining, they set the tone and guidelines for the family. In turn, the tone and guidelines they set influence their children's development in a variety of ways. One important aspect of the child's self-concept, which is influenced by parental behavior, is the child's self-discipline and acceptance of responsibility.

A primary concern of most parents is that they teach their children self-discipline. Highly connected to self-discipline is a positive self-concept because to feel good about oneself one has to have experienced success. Children measure success first by the limits set for them by parents. There is considerable research which shows that children from chaotic families (under-responsible parenting) and rigid families (over-responsible parenting) have low self-esteem as well as difficulty in limiting themselves. Mid-range families, on the other hand, foster high self-worth and personal responsibility. Let's look at ways in which parental discipline and leadership influence the child's self-discipline.

RESPONSIBLE LIMIT SETTING

Teaching self-discipline often occurs in a situation in which parents are called upon to set limits for their children. Consider a twelve-year-old girl who asks whether she can stay out late on a school night because other kids are getting to do it. A parent might respond:

1. "You have to stay in because the police will pick you up since it is past curfew." (Under-responsible—chaotic)
2. "It is not important what other parents let their kids do. Tonight I want you to stay in." (Responsible—flexible or structured)
3. "I want you in at 9:00 every night, no matter what the circumstances." (Over-responsible—rigid)

The key to responsible limit setting is that parents take personal responsibility for the limit being set. In the first example, it appears that the parent's only concern is that the child might get caught. This approach leaves responsibility for enforcement on an outside person or institution with which the child has no relationship. Therefore, the decision to do what she is supposed to is based on the best guess as to whether she will get caught or not.

The parent in the third statement is taking an extreme position and the child knows it. Such a position invites defiance and power struggles. The child can write off this parent as being irrational, but then she is back in the realm of figuring out whether she will be caught or not. The underlying problem is that by closing off all negotiation or discussion, the parent becomes over-responsible for the child. Not only does the child run the risk of losing her own identity but she is not allowed the opportunity to exercise responsibility for her own behavior. The message is that she is not trustworthy.

Neither the under-responsible nor over-responsible response by the parent is conducive to the development of self-discipline. However, the responsible limit-setting response by the parent aids in the child's learning of self-discipline. In the second example, the child has to come to terms with letting down someone whom she cares about by choosing not to comply. Moreover, the person who is setting the limit is not abstract or institutional but personal. Since the child cannot escape or dismiss the responsibility, she has to come to terms with it.

Relationship-based discipline is important in the development of personal integrity. Both chaotic and rigid family structures can produce persons with low self-esteem who make choices on the basis of whether someone will find out or not. If discovered they feel ashamed because they were caught. However, there would be no change in their behavior because in the same situation they would do the same thing again, if there was little chance of being found out. The reason is that in extreme family environments no relationship develops around the limit setting, and the child never internalizes the personal responsibility necessary for true independence.

A strong sense of identity comes with successfully meeting standards coupled with a strong personal relationship. An advantage of relationship-based discipline is that children learn that when they have done something wrong, they can do something to make up for it. Amends can be made because it is personal and not institutional. They are not stuck with loneliness and despair.

The paradox in teaching responsibility and self-discipline is that the effort is not directed first at **making** children be responsible. Rather, as in the second example, the parent accepts responsibility for what is wanted and is not influenced by others. Parents need to take responsibility for the limits they set before they can expect their child to take responsibility for him/herself.

RESPONSIBLE HELPING

Another aspect of parenting with important implications for the development of self-discipline is parental helping. Consider three ways in which a parent may respond to a child's request for help. Brad is a fifth grader who has been having trouble with arithmetic in school. When he asks for help with a page of long-division problems, a parent might respond by saying:

1. "I'm tied up now, Brad, but if you could check with me tomorrow night I might be able to help you." (Under-responsible—chaotic)
2. "Sure, I'd be glad to help. Tell me what you are having trouble with and maybe I can help you figure out how to do these problems." (Responsible—structured or flexible)
3. "If only you'd put more effort in, you'd get it. Now I'll do them and you watch so you can get them right." (Over-responsible—rigid)

In the first response, the parent clearly does not have a sense of the child's need. This is typical of a chaotic family environment. As a consequence, children in chaotic families have no reason to trust that parents will follow through and are convinced they have to do it on their own.

Rev. C. Wayne Perry, Pastor

Their fierce determination to "make it on my own" can result in an extreme self-sufficiency or an extreme sense of failure. When these children become adults, they perpetuate the family inheritance by saying either, "I had to do it the hard way, let them learn" (self-sufficiency), or "I can't handle this" (failure). Thus, the cycle is repeated again.

The third example is typical of a parent's response in a rigid family. Help giving is usually done in an overbearing way, sometimes with an element of ridicule. As a consequence, rigid families foster children who are reluctant to ask for help because the price is too great. With expectations so high and inflexible, to ask for help is perceived as weakness. Help is accompanied by judgment, comparison, and criticism. Parents exploit the vulnerability of asking for help to further shape and influence their children. Even worse is for the parents to solve the problem or do the project themselves to show how it should be done to do it "right." The result is deep embarrassment or shame. It also deprives the child of the opportunity to become responsible for himself by learning through doing.

The second response indicates a willingness to help but a recognition by the parent of limits in giving help. This response is typical of parents in mid-range structured or flexible families. In these families, children feel free to ask for help without feeling judged or criticized. They are confident that parents will respond and do what they say they will but that parents will not take over the project themselves. Parental acceptance of the request without accepting responsibility for the task itself fosters children's self-discipline and responsibility.

Again, we see a paradox in teaching the child self-discipline. The parent's effort is not directed first at making the child be responsible. Rather, the parent accepts responsibility for helping, but s/he does not take over the child's job. Parents need to take responsibility for themselves yet allow their child the opportunity to accept responsibility for him/herself before they can expect the child to do so.

SUGGESTIONS TO PARENTS ABOUT YOUR FAMILY ADAPTABILITY

Understanding a family as a natural system is useful in a number of ways. The family environment experiences changes similar to the seasonal changes found in nature. Chaotic and rigid, relatively flexible and relatively structured periods occur for every family. In fact, most families will vary in their adaptability in different areas of life at the same period in time. For example, a family might be rigid about bedtime and flexible about mealtime.

Issues occur, however, when a family's adaptability does not match the needs of the family members, either adult or children. The greatest risk is becoming stuck in one phase. Being a rigid family all the time would be like having severe winter all year round. As a family, you will have to determine if you do have issues or maybe even a problem of matching your family environment with individual needs. If, as a parent, you decide you have difficulty with a specific aspect of adaptability, here are some suggestions.

For issues of **over-responsible** parenting:

1. Select limited priorities and stand firmly behind them.

   Parents cannot teach everything, so they must establish together what their most important values are. Reflect for a moment on all that you can criticize in a young person's life: personal hygiene and appearance, friends, entertainment, church attendance, table manners, study and work habits, family relationships, dress, T.V. and entertainment choices, leisure time, ad infinitum. Ultimately you cannot do it all. To try is self-defeating and destructive to the relationship. What are the very most important standards to you? Insist on them.

2. Respect one another's individuality.

   Notice how different each family member is. Sometimes being part of a family blurs those differences when it comes to rules and agreements. A helpful concept to remember is the Biblical metaphor

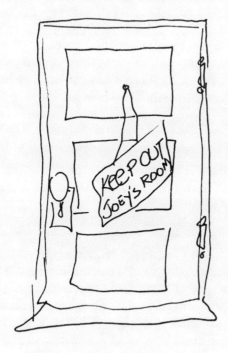

of stewardship in which the steward accepts full responsibility but only for a time. The family environment is a place for adults and children to grow and the "Us" will also change over time.

3. Allow the child to accept consequences for behavior.

Some parents assume responsibility for what kids do when the responsibility really belongs to their children. The pressure needs to remain on the children. The greatest learning of all for the child is to develop the capacity to learn from mistakes.

For issues of **under-responsible** parenting:

4. Keep promises.

To do otherwise is to violate a fundamental trust. A child ought to be able to expect parents to do their best or not make the commitment. It is a standard by which younger people evaluate if they are important or not. Obviously not all agreements can be honored, but those that cannot should be renegotiated.

5. Take personal responsibility for setting limits.

Unpopular decisions based on what others do or say are on shaky ground. External authorities such as the church or school are too abstract and impersonal. When a limit is set, a child will trust it more if it is clear the parent believes in it.

For maintaining **responsible** parenting:

6. Allow the child to meet realistic standards.

Unrealistic standards are the root of low self-worth. Good self-worth depends on the child meeting standards and feeling good about the accomplishment.

7. Praise child for meeting standards.

To only comment on failures or mistakes is to reinforce negative behavior. Acknowledging success is often lost because parents view the child as doing what is expected and reserves special recognition for extraordinary achievements. If only the extraordinary is noticed, children often conclude that negative behavior is a better way to gain parental attention.

8. Live congruently with standards set for children.

The most powerful teaching comes from parents who live the way they ask their children to live. Parents, like children, cannot live up to unrealistic standards, so the capacity to live congruently may be a good index as to how appropriate parental limits are.

9. Invest time in valued activities.

How a parent spends time speaks more loudly than any set of rules or lectures. The values or standards that will be most remembered by a child as s/he grows into adulthood are those which an adult made a personal priority.

By observing these suggestions, parents take on clear responsibility for the leadership and discipline vital to a family's adaptability. Such personal investment heightens the importance of the relationships within the family. It is a greater emotional risk to be truly self-responsible.

FAMILY JOURNAL ENTRY NUMBER ONE   Individual

The family journal is designed to start you reflecting on who you are as a family. It asks a series of questions to which you are invited to respond by either writing notes to each other here on this page or recording in your own private journal. If you respond to another family member's entry, remember there is no right or wrong. It is only a record of what each of you thinks. Take a few minutes to jot down your responses.

1. What are the rules most often discussed in your family?
2. How well does your family accomplish tasks where they have to work together?
3. What happens in your family when there is a crisis?
4. When someone asks for help from other family members, what happens?
5. Are promises kept in your family?
6. If someone in your family broke a rule or an agreement and no one else knew, how would s/he think and feel?

FAMILY ADAPTABILITY PROFILE   **Group**

The purpose of this profile is to encourage discussion among family members. Remember that any family probably fits more than one category. Answer each question by circling the number that you think best describes your family **most of the time.** Then draw a line connecting the circled numbers.

Adaptability Dimension		Rigid	Structured		Flexible		Chaotic	
Leadership	authoritarian	1	2	3	4	5	6	weak
Discipline	strict	1	2	3	4	5	6	permissive
Negotiation	limited	1	2	3	4	5	6	endless
Organized	over-organized	1	2	3	4	5	6	disorganized
Values	inflexible	1	2	3	4	5	6	shifting

Now add up your answers for your Family Adaptability Score: _____

Optional for adults: Go back over the questions and place an X over the number which best describes your family of origin. (If you have difficulty, try to remember your family as it was when you were the age of your own children.) Note if the responses differ from your first answers. Now add up the answers in order to compute your Family-of-origin Adaptability Score: _____

FAMILY CRISIS PROFILE—ADAPTABILITY

Individual/Family

When a family confronts a crisis, there is often a perceptible shift in the family environment. Think of the last time the family faced a crisis. It might have been the death of a loved one, an accident, job loss, illness, moving, spouse returning to an outside job, any change in roles by family members and so forth. Now complete the Adaptability Profile again, but use a state of crisis as the frame of reference. When completed, compare these ratings with your original adaptability profile.

Adaptability Dimension		Rigid	Structured	Flexible	Chaotic	
Leadership	authoritarian	1	2	3	4 5 6	weak
Discipline	strict	1	2	3	4 5 6	permissive
Negotiation	limited	1	2	3	4 5 6	endless
Organized	over-organized	1	2	3	4 5 6	disorganized
Values	inflexible	1	2	3	4 5 6	shifting

Now add up your answers for the Family Adaptability Crisis Score: _____

Optional for adults: Fill out the profile for your family of origin when they were experiencing a crisis. After completing the profile, compare it to your family of origin's typical pattern. If you wish, calculate a Family-of-origin Adaptability Crisis Score: _____

RESPONSIBLE PARENTING INVENTORY—ADAPTABILITY   **Parent**

The following questions are based on the suggestions about adaptability made at the end of this chapter. Respond by circling the number which most accurately represents your answer. There are two columns provided, one for each parent. If there are more adults in the family or there are older children who do some parenting, feel free to use extra sheets.

	First Parent Response:_____	Second Parent Response:_____
1. Do you select limited priorities and stand firmly behind them?	yes 1 2 3 4 5 no	yes 1 2 3 4 5 no
2. Do you respect individual differences?	yes 1 2 3 4 5 no	yes 1 2 3 4 5 no
3. Do you allow your children to accept the consequences of their behavior?	yes 1 2 3 4 5 no	yes 1 2 3 4 5 no
4. Do you keep promises you have made to your children?	yes 1 2 3 4 5 no	yes 1 2 3 4 5 no
5. Do you take personal responsibility for setting limits?	yes 1 2 3 4 5 no	yes 1 2 3 4 5 no
6. Do you allow your child to meet realistic standards?	yes 1 2 3 4 5 no	yes 1 2 3 4 5 no
7. Do you praise your children for meeting standards?	yes 1 2 3 4 5 no	yes 1 2 3 4 5 no
8. Do you live congruently with standards set for children?	yes 1 2 3 4 5 no	yes 1 2 3 4 5 no
9. Do you invest time in valued activities?	yes 1 2 3 4 5 no	yes 1 2 3 4 5 no

LEADERSHIP IN OUR FAMILY   Individual/Family

In most families, different people exert leadership at different times. Dad may lead the family in keeping the yard in order and in planning a vacation. Mom may lead it in terms of organizing household chores, buying clothing and planning meals. Sis may lead the family in preparing for parents' birthdays, making sure everyone has a card and present for Mom or Dad. Brother may lead by getting a game of Monopoly or Scrabble going about once a week. Even little children may lead by making sure everyone is quiet at dinner for a brief prayer before starting to eat.

Spend a few minutes thinking about and sharing how leadership occurs in your family. For each family member, list activities s/he typically leads, if any. Also note those activities for which leadership varies and those for which no leader is readily apparent.

After listing a variety of activities, see if any patterns are evident. Then spend a few minutes talking about your satisfaction with the patterns and whether you might like to change anything.

THE FAMILY INFORMATION TRAIL   **Family**

One way to understand dimensions of a family's life, such as leadership, discipline, negotiation and organization, is to trace how information is shared in the family. When an important decision is made or there is significant news, how do family members hear about it? When you need to know about something, even if it is only to find out when something is happening, who do you ask first? Is there anyone who is always the "last to know?"

To identify how information travels in your family, select a recent "newsworthy" event or decision. Make a diagram tracing how the news was announced and who told whom. Diagram the traveling information as if it were leaving a trail of where it had been. Here's an example:

Billy separately told Mom and Jimmy about something that happened at school. Mom later told Dad and Mary about it at the same time, and Jimmy told Mary at a different time. The diagram might look like this:

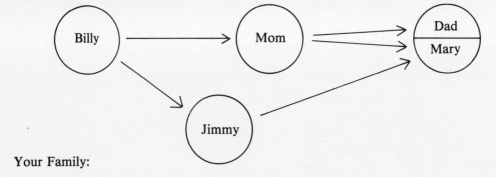

Your Family:

Now decide if this event was a typical pattern in your family. If typical, what implications does it have for your family's adaptability? Some experts consider information as a form of power. Is that power shared in your family to the degree you want it to be?

ASKING FOR HELP IN YOUR FAMILY   Individual/Family

One of the key ways to understand a family's adaptability is to appreciate how help is given in the family. Being dependent on others is an important part of our living together. Make a list of people in your family who regularly need help in some form. Specify the kind of help they need and the types of responses they typically receive. Additional space is left so several people can list their own responses. Reflect on your responses and determine if they are under- or over-responsible. Remember that asking for help occurs for adults as well as for children.

Help Needed By:	Kind of Help:	Response By:	Under-, Over-, Or Self-Responsible:
Example: John needs help with book report.	Proofreading and suggestions for ideas.	Mom: I tend to encourage him to get them in on time and do help him when he has some work done.	Somewhat over-responsible
		Dad: Sometimes I promise to help but then get busy and forget.	Under-responsible
1 .			
2 .			
3 .			
4 .			
5 .			

PARENT PRIORITIES   **Parent**

How flexible parents are around rules and issues is one key to family adaptability. Some parents insist on too many; some on too few. The purpose of this exercise is to help you think about what is most important for you to insist upon in your family. It will also help you recognize if these priorities are reflected in practice.

Part I

In this first part, make a list of the six rules you spend the most energy enforcing. What are the issues that take up your time with your kids?

Rule or Issue

1.

2.

3.

4.

5.

6.

Part II

Now take some time to reflect on your teaching as a parent. What are the things your children will need to learn from you in order to live their lives well? What "lessons," "beliefs," or "principles" do you wish them to remember from their living with you? Make a list of six essential learnings you wish your children to have.

Learning Outcomes

1.

2.

3.

4.

5.

6.

Part III

A family's adaptability is very much affected by what parents insist upon. The rules and organization of a family in many ways are a curriculum in which parents teach. The question for parents is: Are you teaching what you want?

Reflect on the two lists you have made. Is there a difference between where you are putting your energy and time and what you think is the most important? Are your most important learning outcomes appearing in the six rules or issues you enforce? If not, brainstorm a list of possible ways of teaching those outcomes you neglect. Make a list of five concrete steps you can take to achieve a different balance in your teaching as a parent.

Action Steps

1.

2.

3.

4.

5.

STANDARDS FOR KIDS AND PARENTS   **Family**

Sometimes parents set standards for their children which are higher than they hold for themselves. At other times, the standards parents set are much lower than what they expect from themselves. Here we are not talking about achievements such as running a four-minute mile or getting an A average in school. Rather, we are talking about standards in daily life, such as not leaving a mess in their room, getting to places on time, having a neat appearance and so forth.

In the space below, list some areas of daily life, such as personal cleanliness, duties around the house, being on time, etc., in the column at the left. Next jot down standards in your family for parents and for children, then compare the two.

Area of Daily Life	Standards	
	Parents	Children

PLANNING AN ACTIVITY FOR YOUR FAMILY   Children/Family

This exercise is for children only. Plan an activity for your entire family. Try to plan something you haven't done before. Answering the questions listed below will help you develop your plan.

1. What activity have you chosen?

2. What are specifics connected with the activity—where, when, how long it lasts, cost?

3. What preparations are needed for the activity—information to collect, things to be bought or gotten together, reservations or arrangements to be made?

By answering these questions, you have developed a plan for carrying out the activity. Make sure you write down your answers. Also, sometimes it is best to allow two or three options, for example, several different dates for the activity or, perhaps, several ways of making preparations.

When you have developed your plan, talk it over with your parents. Try to develop a firm commitment by all family members to take part in the family activity. This may require that some compromises be made. Before you finish your discussion, however, try to reach agreement on a specific date and time for the activity you have chosen.

CARING

CHAPTER TWO

CARING

As adaptability refers to the basic structure of the family, this chapter describes the cohesive bonds which hold the structure together. Within the loving interchange are the reasons why people join together to form families and stay together. Purpose and identity flow from their common commitments, and for those who miss this commitment in some way, a large void occurs.

For example, I once knew a man who was adopted. He decided he wanted to search for his real mother. He spent many weekends and vacations searching through city archives and tracing leads. He ultimately found her, and all his patience and effort were rewarded. I was impressed with the diligence and commitment that he possessed without any prior relationship with his mother. Even as an adult, his desire to form a connection was profound.

Wanting to know and to have a relationship with your parents is common to all of us. The relationship between parent and child is the first in the child's life and, in that sense, sets precedents for all later relationships. For a parent, it is one of the most intimate relationships in your life, since no one will know your own child as well as you do or know how much you have had to give for the relationship.

The parent-child relationship is a potent one. It even has potency if you did not know your parents, as in the case of my adopted friend. What is not obvious, however, is that the parent-child relationship has impact far beyond any other relationships the child develops. It is also fundamental to how a person makes decisions, accomplishes tasks, and learns from experience. Much of this impact depends on the level and kind of cohesion characterizing a family.

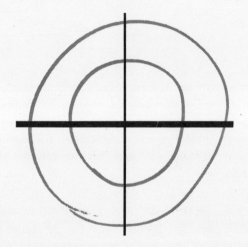

FAMILY COHESION

A family's cohesion is the total of all the caring, closeness, and meaning at the very center of family relationships. Like adaptability, the level and intensity of family cohesion will change with the needs of its members. At times family members will be highly connected and at other times more separated. When children are small, families tend to be more **connected.** Responsibly supportive parents will recognize that children will want less involvement as they mature. With increasing child involvement with peers, parents need to accept the waning of their own influence. These families can be described as more **separated.**

Whether separated or connected, there are five dimensions which are characteristic of a healthy family's cohesion. They are closeness, support, decision making, commonality and unity. Each dimension is critical in how connected or separated a family is.

CLOSENESS

Closeness is a feeling of warmth and care between family members. In more connected families there is a high degree of intimacy. Most of the emotional energy is focused on the family with some outside involvement of family friends. Intense close feelings between parents and children occur most consistently when children are small.

In more separated families, the emotional energy is shared between family and outside friends. Despite outside relationships, such as the teenage peer group, a clear sense of family intimacy remains.

SUPPORT

Support is the affirmation of other family members, especially children. When a person feels vulnerable or dependent, it is critical to receive support. Consequently in a more connected family, where support is more restricted to within the family, parents provide emotional support yet encourage the autonomy and responsible behavior of their children.

More separated families welcome support from outside as well as within the family. As children mature, they are allowed to have different opinions or to be different, yet they have the sustained support of parents. While there is still an emphasis on responsible behavior, family members recognize a number of sources of support for family members.

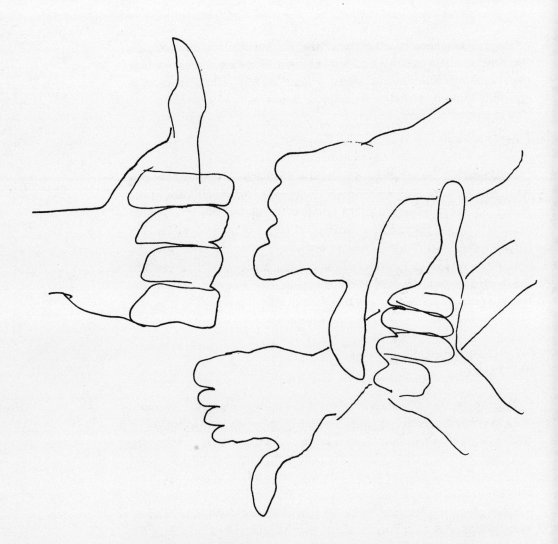

DECISION MAKING

Decision making reflects the level of involvement family members have with one another. A more connected family makes most decisions with the family in mind. Individual choices typically are made in consultation with other family members. A good example is financial decision making. In connected families, most checking and savings accounts are joint accounts with some individual accounts.

By contrast, the more separated family emphasizes individual decisions being made separately though joint decisions are made for whole-family matters. In financial affairs, a separated family relies more on individual accounts as well as some joint accounts. A good metaphor for the independence of an adolescent is when s/he begins to seriously use his/her own bank account.

COMMONALITY

Time, space, interests, activities and friends are some of the things a family can share in common. In a more connected family these are usually shared by most family members. Even individual pursuits, such as a child's soccer or the father's car club, may have high family involvement. The more separated family shares less in common but maintains an emphasis on "family" time and recreation.

Commonality will vary considerably depending on what is shared. Family members may have few friends in common but put a very high priority on spending time together. In thinking about your family, try to discern your patterns in what you do share as a family.

UNITY

Family unity stems from a deep pride in family membership. In more connected families, the meaning attached to family membership is high. Evidence of the importance of traditions, heritage, and beliefs is found in intense efforts to preserve family patterns. Pride is taken in the family name.

More separated families have a moderate sense of unity. While members may find important meaning in being part of the family, there is less emphasis on traditions, beliefs and heritages. There are also fewer efforts to preserve family customs. Separated families may even initiate new traditions. In a culture as diverse and mobile as ours, this is not uncommon.

TO BE CONNECTED OR SEPARATED

All five dimensions have common themes. More connected family members are more involved in each other's lives. More separated families maintain a basic commitment to one another but are open to meeting some of their emotional needs outside the family. These qualities are true of all human organizations. Connection and separateness are both good, depending on how the family is composed and the needs of its members.

There are a number of factors which impact on the cohesion of the family. Age of children is a prime ingredient. Families with young children are usually more connected with parents providing most of the emotional support. Families with older children are typically more separated as children begin to develop bases of support outside the family.

Parental needs are important too. Although most adults have a variety of friends and activities outside the family, nevertheless, their basic source of emotional support and sustenance is still the family. For example, when things are not going well for an adult, support usually is sought from within the family, typically from a spouse or older children. Sometimes even very young children can supply this support, too, through demonstrations of affection or by showing the parent that the child needs him/her. Thus, at times, parents need a more connected environment.

At other times, a more separated environment fits parents' needs better. For example, the mother who is embarking on a career outside the home may need some separation from her family while she sorts out her own goals. A father may need some separation when his career is proceeding well but, at the same time, is placing large demands on his time and energy.

Other factors are also important in determining a family's level of cohesion. The richness of a family's heritage is significant. So is the extent of a family's involvement with relatives on one or both sides. Subcultural norms have a major impact as well. The particular economic situation a family experiences is also important.

Consider the family which works together such as on a family farm or in a family business. They have a broad set of common experiences to share and a rich togetherness. However, if issues occur at work they also become family issues—a fact which can be difficult. To not have shared common experiences is to lose the very basis of intimacy. Yet, too much commonality can create problems as well. Thus, just as with adaptability, cohesion presents the question of whether a family has too much or too little.

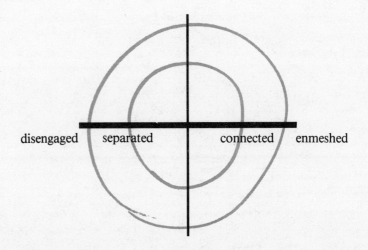

disengaged   separated   connected   enmeshed

TOO CONNECTED OR TOO SEPARATED

Find a partner. Place your palms together and intertwine your fingers so that you have a good grip on one another. Now try to move. Squeeze harder so that you have control over the other. Try again to move. Try to let go. What does it feel like to be so intertwined?

Now, try together another experiment. One of you extends your hands with palms up. The other places their hands carefully on top. Gently rub each other's hands. How is this experience different from the first? Now, the person who has the hands on top should lift them. What does that feel like?

The touching of hands is a physical metaphor for cohesion in the family. The dilemma is how to be close and yet separate. When the fingers are intertwined, it at first feels secure and warm. Yet, when one partner or both tries to move, it is difficult at best. The squeezing pressure may even be painful. At worst, to get free may mean to fight and struggle.

The paradox of every relationship is how to touch and yet not hold on. Like the hands, you can experience the closeness and the freedom to move around if you do not try to control the other. The risk is that the other may leave, and your option is to trust that your partner will not. Trying to control creates a stifling relationship which guarantees the desire to leave. The other possibility is to not touch at all.

Some families end up not touching enough and some become too intertwined. Then issues appear. A teenager whose parents attempt to become part of his gang might well appreciate some separateness. The couple, in which one spouse's career has prevented their spending much time together, may have an issue around connecting.

At times it may be only an adjustment issue. One evening I had dinner with a family who had an unusual dining custom. They told me that one of their issues in blending their customs had to do with eating off each other's plates when dining out. It was customary in the husband's family for members to order different things and then feel free to eat from one another's plate. While he felt his family was too cohesive, he did enjoy

this custom. The wife reported that it was difficult for her to adjust at first, but now she enjoys the custom as well. I too had reservations. After a few pieces of beef were speared off my plate by adventuresome children, however, I decided to join in and had a marvelous time.

Not all cohesion issues are settled so easily. Returning to the metaphor of the hands, it is a basic human question of trust. Trusting enough to be close is one side; not trusting enough to let go is the other. Just as we discovered with adaptability, a family can be over-responsible as well as under-responsible in the giving and sharing of care and support. When under-responsible, a family can become **disengaged.** If over-responsible, the family may become **enmeshed.** If the issues do not become resolved, either extreme can create a problem for the family.

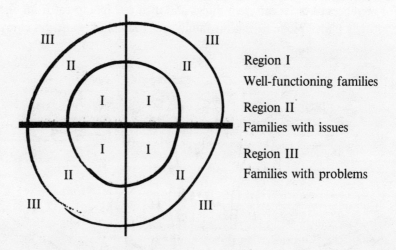

Region I
Well-functioning families

Region II
Families with issues

Region III
Families with problems

UNDER-RESPONSIBLE CARE— THE DISENGAGED FAMILY

In some families the level of cohesion is minimal. These families can be described as engaged. They are more distant than intimate. They are lonely families. Family members see themselves as doing their own thing.

They do not have a lot of interests or friends in common; instead privacy and time apart are emphasized. Members look outside the family to meet emotional needs. One is reminded of the title of David Riesman's 1950's classic book, THE LONELY CROWD.

The heightened sense of independence extends to decision making as well. Since few resources are pooled, there are few decisions requiring family input. Furthermore, there are few traditions and not much of a heritage to pull the family together. Rather this family is characterized by a survivor mentality in which every person fends for him/herself.

One of the contributing factors to disengagement is that closeness is often conditional on doing "right," and parents will withdraw support from children for misbehavior. Have you ever been mad at someone and, rather than be honest, you disconnected from him/her? The other person, sensing the change, asked if anything was wrong. Your response was, "Oh, nothing," but your voice and facial expression continued to convey disapproval. One of our Family Renewal Center mothers described it as "The Look!"

The pattern is common in disengaged families. The real message is this: what you have done threatens our relationship. The distance is maintained as a punishment to insure it does not happen again. When a parent uses this approach with a child, it is particularly threatening. While the focus is on what the child does, the threat is the loss of relationship. Moreover, the parent is not being clear even about the behavior.

The myth that is used to justify this pattern is that one cannot be caring and angry at the same time. In order to be mad, one has to cancel the relationship. This is not true. The people you will be most angry with are the ones you love the most. The opposite of love is indifference, not anger. A disengaged family may look indifferent; but, really, family members are detaching over their issues as opposed to becoming involved deeper in the relationship. Issues are important opportunities for further connection.

Children in disengaged families often feel they have to be perfect in order to maintain the relationship. Knowing they cannot be, they avoid intimacy so as not to get hurt. This may cause their relationships with others to remain shallow and superficial. A painful side effect is that because of their fear of intimacy, they often select marriage partners who have great difficulty in being independent. If they do marry a person who is as self-sufficient as they are, they may elect to be cautious and careful about the other person's significance.

To take full responsibility for one's part in a relationship means being consistently clear about the value of the relationship and the importance of the other person. Without establishing this kind of vulnerability, emotional connection can be difficult. If a couple parallels with their children what happens in their disengaged marriage, the cycle will repeat itself and the disengaged environment can continue for yet another generation.

OVER-RESPONSIBLE CARE—THE ENMESHED FAMILY

The other extreme in family cohesion is called **enmeshed.** In this family, members are over-involved and highly dependent upon one another. No one can be separate without creating anxiety for others. They must spend all their time together and share everything including friends.

Privacy is minimal. Parents know too much about their children and children know too much about their parents. Everyone has to agree on all decisions whether they are personal or family issues. It is as if the family has become one person.

In an enmeshed family, each child is seen as an extension of the parent. Different or wrong behavior is seen as reflecting back on the parents—that they are somehow bad. Parental concerns about their inadequacies tend to blur the responsibility the child has for his/her behavior. The result is that family members are continually concerned about the behavior of other members and how this reflects on them. If you can imagine a small community in which everyone knows everyone else's business, and in which everyone would simply die if an outsider found out something unseemly, you have the picture.

Such relationships become smothering and protective. Autonomy for anyone is difficult. No one can have a separate opinion without that being threatening to the others. Children and adults have a diffuse sense of self in relation to behavior because the boundaries are so blurred. The result is a "my family, right or wrong" attitude. The most extreme form of this attitude is defending a family member no matter what s/he has done. This attitude is expressed in aphorisms such as, "We can say what we like to each other, but no outsider can," or "Hurt one of us, hurt all

of us." The pride in the family is so great that a black eye for one member is seen as a black eye for the whole family. Responsibility for individual behavior is sacrificed for the solidarity of family relationships.

Enmeshed family life is like a soap opera in that it is highly involving in its drama, hard to get out of and, after awhile, it seems like the same old thing. Adults from enmeshed families find other people attractive who have similar difficulty in being separate because it is easy to become over-involved, to take over the other person's responsibility, and to get caught up in the drama. This is how love can become an addiction. In enmeshed families, the main problem is no one can be separate or different and be accepted. Neither parents or children take responsibility for their own behavior because of the involvement of the others. The intensity of the relationships obscures personal boundaries.

RESPONSIBLE PARENTAL CARE GIVING

Children are dependent upon parents for feedback since they have not had the experience to evaluate their own behavior. When they feel rejected at a time when there is a high need for acceptance, it creates an internal civil war within the kid. They can resolve the war in a number of ways including being "super good" or misbehaving to seek attention. A way to avoid the war altogether is for parents to supply acceptance and support in the relationship combined with appropriate limit setting.

There is an essential tension between being supportive and being critical. Parents are asked to supply acceptance which is a key to developing a sense of self-worth. They also must be an evaluator who makes **value** judgments about how a child is doing. This is also a critical factor in developing self-worth. In the previous chapter we learned that the evaluator, limit-setting role could be overdone and underdone. So can parental acceptance and support. It is especially difficult to maintain a balance in both roles. One key to creating balance is in how support is or is not given.

RESPONSIBLE SUPPORTING

Contrast the following three statements by parents who are expressing concern to their child about an upsetting behavior:

1. "Get out of my sight!" (under-responsible—disengaged)

2. "I love you very much, but I cannot accept what you are doing." (responsible—separated or connected)

3. "How could you do this to me?" (over-responsible—enmeshed)

The first statement threatens abandonment or loss of relationship because of the behavior. In a disengaged family, the emphasis is on meeting standards upon which the relationship depends. In statement three, however, the focus is on the relationship. The enmeshed parent takes the child's behavior personally, interpreting it as defiance or as a criticism or judgment of him/her as a parent. The behavior gets lost in the emotional turmoil.

The second statement affirms both limits and the relationship. In mid-range families, a child can make a mistake without the loss of relationship. This is not true of disengaged or enmeshed families. To make a mistake is a shameful experience. In a disengaged family, a child is threatened with abandonment; in the enmeshed family, s/he remains unforgiven. In either situation, the child feels isolated and alone. When the relationship remains intact, however, and the focus is on the limit or standard that has been transgressed, there is a chance to make up for it. Even if the misbehavior was hurtful personally, amends and restitution are possible. Research from many approaches to child rearing shares the common theme of focusing corrective feedback on behavior without threatening loss of relationship. In connected and separated families, parents can separate their relationship with the child from the child's behavior.

Parents can contribute much to a more balanced family environmment by taking responsibility for their own mistakes and errors. Reflect on times that you have blown it with your spouse or children. Maybe it was when you lost the keys to the car many miles from town and somehow made it seem like another person's fault. Or maybe it was when you made a demand of a child which was unreasonable. Even though you may have recognized it later, your pride kept you from admitting it because of the "principle involved."

When parents admit to their own limitations, it avoids the extremes. By taking responsibility for their own behavior, the potential for enmeshment is limited. Accepting behavior as your own is a clear expression of individuality. Similarly, accepting personal responsibility for errors invites support and relationship, thereby limiting the amount of disconnection which occurs. A couple who can have honest differences and remain connected is a significant model for their children. If they maintain the same style of relationship with their children, they create a family climate where children can accept criticism confident that they will not be abandoned. Such a climate fosters development of self-worth, self-discipline, and the capacity to learn from mistakes.

SUGGESTIONS TO PARENTS ABOUT YOUR FAMILY COHESION

The family cohesion climates we described are dynamic and changing. Any family will experience different levels of cohesion at different times, or maybe even in the same day. Moreover, there are times when even the extremes are appropriate. With the birth of a new child, a family needs to be enmeshed. For awhile when circumstances require a family to be split up in different locations, their disconnection will naturally result in seeking relationships with the friends around them.

If a family does get stuck in one phase, it can generate sufficient issues to reach the problem level. Here are some suggestions to overcome the problem.

For issues of **under-responsible** parenting:

1. Spend time with children and together as a family.

A sense of connection requires some time together and some commonality. Some parents only interact with their child when something is wrong. Given the rush of modern life, unless something is causing a problem, the child may not get attention. To not be overlooked, one has to cause trouble. A positive parent relationship is based on the parents wanting such a relationship. Time together is a barometer of this desire.

2. Allow children to make mistakes.

To be able to make a mistake means you do not have to be perfect. Mistakes are opportunities for learning and promote good conscience development. To suffer being put-down or being discredited for your error is to make more than a mistake out of it. It is a clear message of non-acceptance.

For issues of **over-responsible** parenting:

3. Allow children to have a different opinion or be different.
There is much research which confirms that it contributes developmentally to a child when they are allowed to hold opinions and attitudes contrary to the parents. This is not to suggest that parents alter goals or limits but that they validate the feelings and beliefs of their offspring by hearing them out.

4. Allow children to accept consequences for behavior.

Some parents work too hard and assume responsibility for what children do that really belongs to their children. The pressure needs to remain on the children. The greatest learning of all for the child is to develop the capacity to learn from mistakes.

For maintaining a climate of **responsible** parenting:

5. Work for a relationship which is close yet encourages autonomy of the child.

Statements such as, "I wish she could stay just the way she is," reflect a longing most parents have. The reality is, however, our job as parents is to develop self-sufficiency while maintaining a sense of security. This means that as a child matures, parents encourage the development of interests and friends apart from the family.

6. Criticize the behavior and not the person.

"Why is it whenever there is trouble around here, you are in the middle of it," is clearly a personal criticism. It is vital that the child be supported to assist him in the ownership of counter-productive behavior. Bad behavior does not mean the loss of parent care. Nor does it mean the child is bad.

7. Admit mistakes.

Parents do not have to be perfect either. They can model self-acceptance and promote child respect by not trying to be more than human. Also, children will more readily accept responsibility for their own behavior, if they see adults doing it. Parents who fear they will lose their authority might consider the origin of the word "author" which connotes life-giving creativity.

By acting upon these suggestions, parents accept clear responsibility for giving emotional support to their children. Parents who are appropriately supportive strive for a solid relationship with their children, but they also try to set limits to help their children develop self-discipline and a sense of self-worth. Thus, responsible parenting requires that attention must be given to both a family's adaptability and its cohesion. Both are vital to the personal development of the child and to the adult's development as well.

In these first two chapters, two major dimensions of a family's functioning were discussed. On each dimension several family "models" were described. These models are intended to help create better understanding of families. Remember, however, that the models are just that; in real life there are no "pure" enmeshed, disengaged, chaotic, or rigid families.

In the next chapter, the two dimensions are put together in a Family Map™. Using the Family Map, you will be able to understand where you currently are as a family. Some further ideas will be introduced to help you better understand the directions you may be going as a family. Where you are now and where you are going both depend to some extent on where you have been as a family. Your understanding of your family may be critical to where you will appear on your map.

THE BLENDING OF TWO EPICS

Becoming a family is essentially the blending of two epics. Each parent brings to the marriage a conscious history and an unconscious heritage forming a powerful tradition. The traditions represent a complex mosaic of past strivings, sufferings, learnings, and successes. They are taught to each generation as symbolic of what has become valued and meaningful. The decision as to how the traditions are to be blended and then shared with the offspring is highly significant. Yet, most of us do it unconsciously.

The public's fasination with Alex Haley's work, **ROOTS,** betrays our fascination with family epics. No longer is the family tree the preserve of the amateur historian. Many are now exploring their families of origin as a way of learning about themselves and being conscious of the decisions they are currently making. A family's roots take shape in central decisions about marriage and children. It all starts at the very first meeting.

FIRST MEETING

Within the first four minutes of a couple's first meeting, fundamental aspects of their relationship are already established. In fact, some family therapists ask a couple to describe their first date as a way to initiate therapy. The importance of their first meeting is historic because it is when the two family epics first touch. It sets a tone and sometimes becomes the key to the whole relationship. At minimum, a couple will use it as a common reference point for their life together. Whether you are an adult or a younger person, it is important that your parents have shared with you their first meeting. If you do not know it, it is like reading a story without knowing how it began.

ESTABLISHING A SYSTEM

Once a couple has decided to pursue a relationship together, they face a fundamental decision. The choice has to do with what kind of system they will have. Will it be like his or like hers? Or will they negotiate a compromise solution which blends the best of both or maybe even a unique solution which is unlike either family of origin.

Referring back to the phases of adaptability can provide perspective on this choice making. For example, let's look at a man from a relatively rigid family and a woman from a pretty chaotic family. He may be first attracted to her because of her easy-going, quixotic manner. Similarly, she might admire his sense of certainty and determination. Everything is fine until they have to make some decision together. Then suddenly he may be perceived as stubborn and she regarded by him as "flakey." Now their choices are:

1. They can operate in a rigid, tight manner as his family did, probably with him calling the shots.
2. They can survive "catch as catch can" as her family did, probably with her setting the tempo.
3. They can negotiate a more balanced system—either the structured or flexible—which enhances desirable qualities of both, is different than either family, and involves both of them in the process.

There is another possibility. They might decide not to decide. Some couples spend entire marriages struggling over whose way is right. Their relationship is usually characterized by self-righteous fault finding and blame. In our example, he remains steadfastly convinced that families should be run in a rigid fashion while she refuses to be tied down to an arbitrary set of rules. In the final analysis they both really share a problem since every choice that comes up presents a potential conflict. Conflicts such as:

— how do finances get handled?

— how do household chores get distributed?

— how are children to be raised?

— what time to go to bed? get up?

— what kind of church community to belong to?

— who friends should be?

— who sleeps on what side of the bed?

— whose job is it to put on the morning coffee?

— who is supposed to initiate affection?

— how clean is clean?

— what should the thermostat be set at?

— whose turn is it to...?

The couple who has not decided how they are going to be together faces potential crisis and conflict in each issue. For the undecided, it is an ongoing civil war. Some of these issues are tough even for people who come from identical systems.

THE RELATIVE TEST

One way to check out a relationship for this conflict is to take what I call the **relative test.** How do you react to your partner's relatives? Do you enjoy them even though they are different or, in your opinion, even a little off the wall? Or, is it hard to be with them? Do you find yourself

critical and wishing you did not have to spend time with them? If you feel comfortable, you probably are not threatened by your partner's family since as a couple you have resolved how your family system is going to operate.

However, if you notice parallels between your
partner and aspects of the family you
do not like
and
if you point out how s/he is just like his/her
mother (father) or comment that s/he "might
become like" her/him
and
if you offer a detailed analysis to your partner
about why their family is really crazy
and
if you secretly think that your partner does the
same crazy things
and
if you hope your criticism will get your spouse
to change,
then
you may have an "epic" problem.

It is a sure sign that you and your partner have not decided on how your system is going to run.

Relatives can make this difficult. A couple might find their relationship very workable, but their families may withhold approval. Any couple whose relationship costs them their families' support knows how punishing this experience can be. Shakespeare described this conflict well in the famous feud between the Montagues and the Capulets which resulted in the death of their children, Romeo and Juliet. He concluded,

There never was a story of more woe
than this of Juliet and her Romeo.

The point is that all couples have to negotiate through their respective family traditions. Both families have an enormous investment in all that has happened thus far. To begin a new episode in the epic is significant.

BIRTH OF CHILDREN

Nothing brings out the issues embedded in family tradition more clearly than the birth of a child. As in marriage, some of the very earliest expectations become the most powerful. What meaning the birth of a child has for each parent can be the foundation of future family dynamics and can sometimes become a burden for the child. A child who is expected to be a high achiever or to pull the marriage together can have a tough go of it within the family.

In writing this chapter, I started to wonder about my early perceptions of my own children. I searched through old papers and journals and found this excerpt written about my son, David, on his first birthday.

> David has light blond hair, weighs just under thirty pounds, and possesses six teeth—the last being disconcerting considering that I had just become used to him not having any. Among his accomplishments are the recognition of a few words, the capacity to walk albeit at times unsteady, and a remarkable dexterity in his hands whether it be grabbing for mama's plant, stringing the toilet paper into the living room or removing the mechanical drain plug from the bath tub. David does not speak as yet, utilizing a ready smile at the simplest of joys or perhaps a wrapping of his arms around your neck at the fears of the night to express feelings that need not be verbalized. In fact, that ability underlines one of his most striking features: that at age one he knows those essential things that all men must learn—and yet continually forget—for implicit in his actions is the knowledge that nothing else makes any sense unless you love someone.

> And nothing seems to escape his notice. I do not know how many times I have repeated the story about David picking up the small gray stone in the driveway and intensely examining its every feature for a seemingly unending period of time. When I looked at it, I realized that stone had always been there, but I had never noticed it, and yet David was quite right; it was an interesting stone. Everything within his reach—whether it be leaves, flowers, or the vacuum cleaner—comes under the same searching scrutiny. Maybe

it is a matter of perspective. I remember Robert Rurak's great insight when he described the old man saying to the boy, "even a bedbug is pretty if you look at it right." And as someone close recently suggested to me, the reason for David's uninhibited joy is that he brings no assumptions or prejudices to the things he looks at.

His curiosity and involvement with his world are probably not unique to him as a baby. Yet, even his father, according to family legend, would spend unnumbered hours gazing at a Christmas tree. Moreover, I know that my father, despite outward appearances of pragmatic and businesslike attitudes, is and always has been an inveterate dreamer. If this is part of David's heritage, his vision is bound to be accompanied by life's given measures of disillusionment as well as success—as it was in his father's and his grandfather's.

Therein is the core of parental anxiety—the certainty that David will have to learn to cope by himself with those disappointments which naturally come to the open, the curious, and the seeking. But this concern is tempered by an equal confidence that not only do our experiences affect us, but we are molded and remolded by those who love us and accept without reservations our process of becoming.

What struck me as I recall that passage, is that the meaning—or set of beliefs—that one brings to the watching of one's children will be part of the perception itself. What I had written was as much a commentary on me and my father as it was on David. I watched him with an intergenerational continuity. Our memories of the past extend into the hopes of the future.

During the Italian Renaissance, families maintained archives to collect letters, journals, diaries and family records and would often chronicle the major happenings. We do the same but in a more unconscious way. We all know the stories that are repeated over and over again in sort of an oral tradition. In my family I know:

— that I have great-grandparents from Sweden who were born in Skåne and great-grandparents from County Cork and Dublin in Ireland.

— that while my Scotch-Irish ancestors were struggling through the South in Arkansas and Missouri I had Irish predecessors in the North including one who was one of the Union officers to accept Lee's surrender at Appomattox.

— that the depression of the 1930's left deep scars in my family and how my parents struggled to get out of it by starting a dog business.

— that the stillborn death of the first child in my family affected how my parents viewed my birth as the second.

— that I have often struggled with the irony that my son, David, has two grandparents who served in World War II—one as a German officer in the Nazi Wehrmacht in Belgium and the other as an American G.I.

— that the closest our family ever was was when we all worked together running the family kennel while my dad started his new career.

I could go on for pages, as you might about your family. Events which are talked about, relived and retold combine to form the family legend. The meaning I make of them I bring to every new event, whether conscious or not. They are my "roots." They are part of my identity as a person and our "Us" concept as a family.

It is little wonder, then, that family relationships have so much intensity. So much is at stake as two powerful traditions join together in marriage and family life. The intensity continues as the family grows. This growth has important significance for each individual family member as we shall see in the next chapter, "Growing."

FAMILY JOURNAL ENTRY NUMBER TWO   **Individual/Family**

This entry is concerned with the bonds that unite a family. As in the first entry, you are invited to share your reactions to the following questions.

1. If you had only two stories out of your family's history to pass on to the next generation, which ones would they be?
2. What happens in your family if someone makes an unpopular decision?
3. When someone makes a mistake, what do other family members do?
4. How are decisions made in your family?
5. What activities and interests do family members have in common?
6. Do family members have space in your home to be alone?
7. What is a symbol of the pride your family takes in being a family?
8. What questions have you always wanted to ask your parents about the family history?

FAMILY COHESION PROFILE   **Group**

The purpose of this profile is to encourage discussion among family members. Remember that any family probably fits more than one category. Answer each question by circling the number that you think best describes your family **most of the time.** Then draw a line connecting the encircled numbers.

Cohesion Dimension	Disengaged			Separated	Connected	Enmeshed		
Closeness	not close	1	2	3	4	5	6	too close
Support	none	1	2	3	4	5	6	too much
Decision making	only individual	1	2	3	4	5	6	family only
Commonality	little	1	2	3	4	5	6	everything
Unity	none	1	2	3	4	5	6	total

Now add up your answers for your Family Cohesion Score: _____

Optional for adults: Answer the questions again, placing an X over the number which best describes your family of origin. (If you have difficulty, try to remember your family as it was when you were the age of your own children.) Note if the responses differ from your first answers. Now add up the answers in order to compute your Family-of-origin Cohesion Score: _____

FAMILY CRISIS PROFILE—COHESION   Individual/Family

Families often experience changes in their support and closeness when confronted with a crisis. Think of the last time the family faced a crisis. It might have been the death of a loved one, an accident, job loss, illness, moving, spouse returning to an outside job, any change in roles by family members, etc. Complete the Cohesion Profile again, but use a state of crisis as the frame of reference.

Cohesion Dimension	Disengaged	Separated	Connected	Enmeshed
Closeness	not close 1	2 3	4 5	6 too close
Support	none 1	2 3	4 5	6 too much
Decision making	only individual 1	2 3	4 5	6 family only
Commonality	little 1	2 3	4 5	6 everything
Unity	none 1	2 3	4 5	6 total

Now add up your answers for your Family Cohesion Crisis Score: _____

Optional for adults: Answer the questions again, placing an X over the number which best describes your family of origin. (If you have difficulty, try to remember your family as it was when you were the age of your own children.) Note if the responses differ from your first answers. Now add up the answers in order to compute your Family-of-origin Cohesion Crisis Score: _____

RESPONSIBLE PARENT INVENTORY—COHESION   Parents

The following questions are based on the suggestions about cohesion made at the end of this chapter. Respond by circling the number which most accurately represents your answer. There are two columns provided, one for each parent. If there are more adults in the family or there are older children who do some parenting, feel free to use extra sheets.

Inventory Questions:	First Parent Response:_____	Second Parent Response:_____
1. Do you spend time with your children?	yes 1 2 3 4 5 no	yes 1 2 3 4 5 no
2. Are you supportive when your children make mistakes?	yes 1 2 3 4 5 no	yes 1 2 3 4 5 no
3. Do you accept your children when they have a different opinion or act differently than you would?	yes 1 2 3 4 5 no	yes 1 2 3 4 5 no
4. Do you allow your children to accept the consequences of what they do and not protect them?	yes 1 2 3 4 5 no	yes 1 2 3 4 5 no
5. Do you support your children developing their own interests?	yes 1 2 3 4 5 no	yes 1 2 3 4 5 no
6. When you have an issue, are you critical of behavior and not the person?	yes 1 2 3 4 5 no	yes 1 2 3 4 5 no
7. Do you admit your mistakes?	yes 1 2 3 4 5 no	yes 1 2 3 4 5 no

FAMILY SUPPORT   Individual/Family

Draw a diagram of who supports whom in your family. In the diagram the distance of lines shows how far people are from one another. In every family support is given to different members in different amounts at different times. Use arrows to show direction of support. For example, consider the following family:

In this family Grandma spends a lot of time supporting Mom around the house and taking care of the kids. Mom and Dad support one another and Erin who is still a toddler. They also support John but not as much since he is much older. A diagram for this family would look like this:

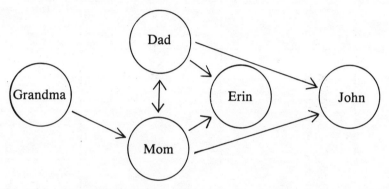

Make a similar picture of your family. You may wish to use a separate piece of paper. If people are not supporting each other in ways you would like, then also draw an **ideal** diagram to show how you would like support to be given in your family.

If each person in the family makes his/her own diagram (real and ideal), have a discussion in the family comparing their different perceptions. Then, together, draw one diagram which shows what the ideal family support network would look like for your family. Keep it so you can look at it again at the conclusion of the book.

FAMILY COMMONALITY   **Family**

Explore together what you have in common as a family and what you have separately as individuals. Use the following chart as a way to itemize friends, activities and interests that two or more family members have in common and those that are separate. After completing the list, have a discussion focusing on these questions: Is there balance between family and individual activities? Does each individual in the family have some individual interests and activities? Is everyone included in the family-together time?

In Common	Friends	Activities	Interests
Separate (list each family member separately)	Friends	Activities	Interests

THE BIGGEST MISTAKE I EVER MADE: **Family**
A FAMILY CONVERSATION

Hold a family conversation in which each person talks about "the biggest mistake I ever made." As each person talks, the rest of the family needs to take special care to listen and to avoid put-downs. By accepting one another, even after making a mistake, you will notice the special bonds which unite your family together. This kind of conversation may foster greater generosity within the family towards each other's shortcomings.

A HERITAGE CHECK LIST   Individual/Family

The following is a list of activities a family might pursue in order to preserve its heritage. As you read through them, place an X in front of those you currently are doing and place a ✔ in front of those you might like to do.

_____ 1. Have a regular story-telling time as a family.

_____ 2. Conduct a "story search" by asking all the relatives for stories they can remember.

_____ 3. Construct a family tree which records careers, life spans, deaths and special events in your family's history.

_____ 4. Develop a family archive for diaries, letters and clippings.

_____ 5. Tape interviews with family elders.

_____ 6. Make sure all old pictures are labeled and in order.

_____ 7. Write letters to children now as a way of preserving images of their childhood.

_____ 8. Make an annual family journal of all the major events in the family's year.

_____ 9. Start a regular filing system of all children's mementos.

_____ 10. Keep a personal diary or journal about the family.

_____ 11. Locate old records (city, church, newspaper, etc.) about the family's history.

_____ 12. Find out where some of your ancestors are buried and visit the sites.

_____ 13. Create a collection of old family possessions (books, Bibles, albums, jewelry, furniture, clothes, etc.).

Other things your family does or that you can think of.

_____ 14.

_____ 15.

_____ 16.

Which suggestions could you start now? List their number here:

FAMILY TRADITIONS AND RITUALS   Individual/Family

In the blending of epics, every family carries on traditions and rituals of the previous generations plus adds some of their own. To appreciate that process in your family, complete the following chart and questions.

Rituals and Traditions from Mom's Family	Rituals and Traditions from Dad's Family	New Rituals and Traditions We have Started
1.	1.	1.
2.	2.	2.
3.	3.	3.
4.	4.	4.
5.	5.	.5.
6.	6.	6.

1. In looking at the chart, are there traditions or rituals that are not being preserved in your family which you wish were?
2. Are there any new traditions or rituals which you would like to start?
3. What contributions can the kids make to your family's heritage?

FAMILY STORIES   **Family**

If you have enjoyed sharing stories as part of UNDERSTANDING US, here are some ideas to generate further story telling in your family.
1.   What stories do children remember about living with parents?
2.   What is the funniest thing each person remembers that has happened in the family?
3.   What is the scariest thing family members remember?
4.   What is the hardest thing the family has ever had to do?
5.   When did family members miss the rest of the family the most?
6.   What is the saddest moment you have shared as a family?
7.   What are some dreams you have had while sleeping that can be shared?.

COUPLE'S CONFLICT SURVEY   **Parents**

Many of the issues that couples face are rooted in their adaptability, cohesion or blending of families. Select five issues that seem to come up over and over again in your relationship. For each, determine if it is an adaptability problem, a cohesion problem or an epic problem (i.e., a difference in how each person's family of origin approached the issue). Make a check in the appropriate column.

Areas of Disagreement	Adaptability Problem	Cohesion Problem	Epic Problem
1.			
2.			
3.			
4.			
5.			

First, you may notice that more than one column was checked in a number of areas. Also, it is possible that one column may have been checked consistently. If a pattern emerges, compare your survey with your adaptability and cohesion profiles. For instance, do any of the specific dimensions, such as negotiation or decision making, help you to understand how you perceive a problem differently? Do you observe any parallel patterns in your family-of-origin ratings? Set some time aside and discuss the patterns surrounding the issues. Avoid trying to resolve the issues. Focus, rather, on the process of how you end up conflicted. Then select one issue and see if perspective has changed your perception of the problem.

GROWING

CHAPTER THREE

GROWING

Families change. As children grow, they require different types of help from their parents. The family that has three children under the age of eight will be organized very differently from the same family when all three children have graduated from high school. How the family handles these transitions will be significant for the well being of every family member. The quality of married life will be substantially affected by parenting. Similarly, children will carry the imprint of the family throughout their adult lives. The family is the first school in which we learn about relationships, values and decision making. It is also where each of us is first confronted with growth and change. This chapter focuses on the process of growth as it occurs in the family environment.

Our popular notions often create an image of the family as stable and secure. However, any parent who has weathered the fear of a child's first day at school, the pangs of adolescence, or the exuberance of high school graduation knows clearly that being in a family is far from being static. Adults too experience developmental crises, such as the "empty nest" syndrome or forty-year-old "middlescence." Additional stresses occur in the contemporary family such as career change for either mother or father, the death of grandparents or the disruptive transfer to another part of the country. Finally, there are few families which are not affected by untoward events such as sickness, divorce or alcoholism. Thus, almost by definition, to be in a family means to be changing and growing.

As we have seen, cohesion and adaptability are key to a family's growth. Taken together they form a "map" by which a family's growth can be traced. The Family Map™ is a useful way to discuss changes in the family and how change affects individual members.

THE FAMILY MAP

Imagine a map which instead of using longitude and latitude uses adaptability and cohesion. North/south represents the dimension of adaptability and east/west represents cohesion.

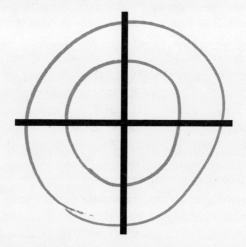

The Family Map also has regions. Each region represents some combination of adaptability and cohesion. The central regions (Region I and II), which are by far the most populated, reflect the more moderate levels of adaptability—structured and flexible—and the more moderate levels of cohesion—connected and separated. Unlike the central regions, Region III is characterized by extremes. As a result, few families remain in Region III for any length of time. Any family may find itself anywhere on the Family Map at some point in time, so it is important to be able to understand the difference between regions.

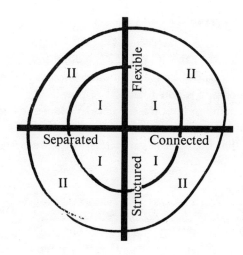

REGIONS I AND II —
THE AREA OF FAMILY WELLNESS

Region I is the area of greatest wellness. Families in this region have achieved the most balanced solutions, given the age and growth of their members. These families typically operate in the mid-range of the various aspects of adaptability (flexible/structured) and cohesion (separated/connected). There are five aspects of wellness which typify families in Region I: collaboration, parenting, problem solving, environment, and an "Us" concept. Each aspect involves a sub-dimension of both adaptability and cohesion:

Adaptability		**Cohesion**
Leadership	Collaboration	Closeness
Discipline	Parenting	Support
Negotiation	Problem Solving	Decision Making
Organization	Environment	Commonality
Values	"Us" Concept	Unity

COLLABORATION

Collaboration is the capacity to get a job done and feel good about being together doing it. Strong leadership roles foster initiative. Each person feels affirmed and is able to accept responsibility for his/her part in the family. All members have the capacity to adapt and change, yet family commitment creates a sense of balance and normalcy. Family members trust that their needs and wants will be respected.

PARENTING

Parenting involves setting appropriate limits while maintaining positive support. Parents are dependable, realistic, and clear. They recognize that children may not be dependable, realistic, or clear as a natural part of their developmental growth. Parenting often involves accepting that younger people make mistakes and need help but that they may not wish to acknowledge either. Effective parenting requires parents to acknowledge that the same may be true for themselves. The hardest part of parenting is allowing an emerging child to be different from parental preconceptions.

PROBLEM SOLVING

Problem solving starts with the assumption that conflict is neither good nor bad; rather it is simply inevitable. Family members have the capacity to achieve agreement by involving themselves in making choices and in seeking solutions. Each person feels assured of his/her personal value and is confident s/he will not be left out. This confidence allows for a high tolerance of conflict and a willingness to examine many options and solutions. Families with effective problem solving deal with issues as they occur and do not allow tensions to build up. The result is that choices are optimal and have an excellent chance of being implemented.

ENVIRONMENT

In many ways the environment reflects the implemented choices of the family. Environmental wellness is the result of a family's ability to be prepared and orderly while taking account of both common and individual interests. Basic to the healthy environment is a sufficient shared experience to sustain intimacy yet foster individuality. Family members are aware of their interdependency, and they take initiative to plan against stress and fragmentation. Concrete evidence of environmental success is a family that consistently spends time together.

"US" CONCEPT

Like the self-concept, a family "Us" concept is rooted in a solid value system which is supported by members having a high sense of purpose and meaning in being together. Common struggles, heritage and beliefs are at the core of the value system. They serve as common standards of value and achievement. Often there is a sustained spiritual base to the value system. Fundamental to the "Us" concept is an awareness and pride in the family as an ongoing unit. It is strongest when all members are highly committed.

REGION II

Families often shift from Region I to Region II when pressure for change develops. The pressure may occur because of factors either inside or outside the family. Issues then arise which may create tension and conflict in the family. Although the natural tendency for families is to resist change, the shift to Region II provides an excellent opportunity for creatively restructuring the family system. Typically the issues which arise as the family structure shifts signal a need for change to better accommodate individual family members or external circumstances.

Region II of the Family Map mostly parallels Region I. A family in Region II usually has some issue or issues in one aspect of wellness that remains unresolved. This need not be serious since on the other dimensions the family does well. In fact, it may only require some adjustment to achieve a new balance. The family needs to focus on its issues in order to maximize a nurturing environment. However, if there are many issues that are difficult to resolve, a family may be bordering on Region III.

REGION III

Region III is an environment that is not as supportive or effective as it needs to be. To be in this region means that a family is experiencing difficulty in almost all aspects of wellness. Family members will have to supply a high level of energy and concentration to bring about change. The family may need help in order to move on the map.

There are four particularly extreme types of families which occur in Region III: chaotic disengaged, chaotic enmeshed, rigid disengaged, rigid enmeshed. The descriptions of these families which follow are scenarios of the kinds of issues families would confront in different parts of Region III. Obviously, few families fit any of these pure types.

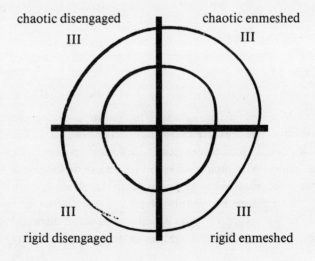

CHAOTIC DISENGAGED

Finding this kind of family is hard since by definition there is little to hold it together. There is no structure or order, nor are there the emotional bonds necessary to sustain family life. It is as if the family is possessed by a centrifugal force which in its spinning around pushes family members out and away from the family. It is theorized that this type of family is one of the major sources of adolescent runaways in this country.

Because the family is in a state of disintegration, family members find it difficult to get things done. People go their separate ways. Limits are not set for the children who, instead, are left on their own at an early age. Members walk away from their problems preferring to follow their separate interests instead of facing their collective problems. The constant state of transition allows everyone the freedom to do his/her own thing. As a family, there is little valuable or meaningful in being together.

CHAOTIC ENMESHED

The force in this family is centripetal, not centrifugal. Like the chaotic disengaged, the chaotic-enmeshed family also spins. Family members, however, are drawn into a vortex of family problems which are complex and insurmountable. It is like a soap opera: everyone knows everybody else's business, and it is difficult to remain uninvolved. Despite the constant energy drain, it is difficult to leave.

Unable to get things done, family members remain highly dependent upon one another. Parents fail to set limits which results in role reversals on the part of children who feel that someone has to do something.

Parents, children, and spouses start to act as if they were one person. Problems pile up resulting in a sense that the family is in a constant state of crisis. The family is very significant to its members but has few values to give direction. Consequently, family members often rely on external standards and even circumstances to make decisions.

RIGID DISENGAGED

Often these families are families in name only, more form than substance. Highly organized and even bureaucratic, they lack emotional involvement. Relationships are empty, devoid of vulnerability, care and feeling. Members often feel constrained to keep up pretenses even though relationships are unrewarding. Transitional phases, such as the empty-nest period, are particularly difficult because they accentuate personal loneliness.

Objectives are met because members are supposed to meet them, not because they care for one another. Expectations are high, especially for children, and conformity is required if members are to be considered part of the family. Family members have little input into negotiations so decisions are usually made by individuals alone. The family possesses very stringent values but shares few experiences to make life together as a family meaningful.

RIGID ENMESHED

The rigid-enmeshed family often has an exaggerated sense of family honor. To challenge a family decision or value is seen as having stained the whole family, and this behavior is taken very personally. This creates problems since the family code is usually pretty elaborate. To make it even more difficult, the family lacks the flexibility to resolve the issues. Instead these families often pretend that an issue is not really an issue. Members who raise issues are made to feel crazy. In this way, the family maintains its code.

Life the Mafia, the rigid-enmeshed family can be ruthless in meeting family objectives at the expense of the members. Extremely high expectations are shared intergenerationally. Limited negotiations result in decision making by fiat, but all members are expected to support decisions. Preparations and plans are backed with such harsh consequences that there is little room for individual initiative in crisis. Underlying the family's inflexibility is a complex value system which is seen as extremely important to the survival of the family.

EXPLORING THE FAMILY MAP

In order to explore the various regions of the Family Map, you first assess where you are now as a family. You can do that using the cohesion and adaptability profiles you completed in Chapters One and Two. It has been most successful if parents first carefully discuss the Family Map together and then share their findings with their offspring. Single parents can achieve similar results by seeking the assistance of an adult close friend who knows the family well. In either event, these family conversations promote a more complete appreciation of how families develop. They also foster a much deeper understanding of one another which is the central goal of the program.

Begin by setting aside a specific time to explore your results. After you have agreed upon a time, take the following steps:

1. Complete the Family Map exercise at the end of the chapter.
2. Read the remainder of this section, especially the suggestions on the next few pages.
3. Discuss the results with each other.
4. Share the results with your children in Session III of UNDERSTANDING US or in a family meeting.

UNDERSTANDING THE FAMILY MAP

In the previous two sessions, you were asked to rate your family on the profiles for cohesion and adaptability. You may have had difficulty specifying a single position on each dimension. For example, you may have seen your family as falling at several points on a sub-dimension of adaptability such as leadership. Recognize that even though you came up with a single score on each dimension of the Family Map, your family does not occupy just one small point on the Map. Rather, your family probably fits in a small **area** of the Family Map. It is best to think of yourself as a small circle on the Map about the size of a nickel, not just a single point.

Different family members will have different views of the family. If they are fairly close together, most of them will fit in roughly the same area of the Map, indicating that all of you see your family in pretty much the same way. Sometimes, however, various family members have considerably different views of the family. These differences, as well as difficulties you may encounter in rating your family, can be caused by a number of factors:

1. **Situations can induce extreme responses.** Some issues, such as sexuality, rebellion, dishonesty, and the like, are so emotionally charged and value laden that they can bring some extreme form of response from the family. These will stand out in your memory but may not reflect the characteristic behavior of your family.

2. **Stress or change can alter the family environment.** Divorce, death, job change, moving—all are stressful events which can create chaos

or rigidity, as well as relationship dislocations. One of the most stressful events to occur within the family is a child becoming an adolescent. The consequence of stress is that recent behavior may be very different from what happened before the event.

3. **Tension between spouses will intensify extremes.** Power struggles over an issue in the marriage tend to create extreme positions. The resulting tension may result in very different perceptions of behavior within the same family.

4. **Children's developmental stages can diversify the family environment.** A family which has pre-school children as well as teenagers is hard to evaluate because of the different needs of the children.

5. **Chaotic families are capable of diverse and changing responses.** It is the nature of chaotic families to be constantly shifting in their patterns. They are fully capable of alternately being enmeshed and disengaged at the same time.

6. **Memories of crises can affect perceptions of family members.** A family may respond to a crisis differently than they respond on a day-by-day basis. However, in our memory, it is the crisis which will stand out. It is helpful to know how a family responds to a stressful situation, in order to maintain clarity about its normal functioning.

7. **Stages of adult growth will influence the family environment.** As adults grow and change, their needs for family flexibility and closeness may also be altered. If their needs are considerably different from the rest of the family, their perceptions will often be different as well.

8. **Unresolved issues in the "blending of epics" can create divergence within the family.** Spouses coming from different types of families handle situations differently if they have not worked out a common system of their own. It is useful to check out the influence of each parent's family of origin.

9. **Any event witnessed by a number of people will result in different versions.** Nowhere is this more true than in the family where each witness has a high investment in the outcome. This is one of the central difficulties in the "scientific" measurement of family life. It is also an issue for families in resolving their own differences.

Finally, it is important for you to see the Family Map for what it is—a map and not a test. It is simply a way to think about your family and to share your perceptions with other family members. There are tests available which your instructor may ask you to take if you are enrolled in an UNDERSTANDING US Program. The Map in this book is designed to assist in sharing perceptions which offer a family insight about themselves.

The most successful way to discuss the Map is to allow each other differences of perception. It is not necessary to prove the adequacy of your perception. It is indispensible to hear each other out since our perceptions affect our behavior. Respecting each other's differences also reflects a basic part of family life. How individuals grow is affected by the responses other family members make. Family growth patterns are, in turn, affected by the emerging roles of individual family members.

Consider your Family Map. Did your scores tend to cluster in one region or were there great differences in perception? Think how the scores would have been altered if your family had used the Map four years ago. Chances are there would have been differences between your current scores and those of four years ago. Sooner or later all families tend to diverge as family members mature and develop. The key ingredient to this growth, whether adult or child, is the search for identity. Without understanding the role which identity plays in personal development, it is difficult to appreciate how a family evolves. This is the focus of the second part of this chapter, the Identity Cycle.

THE IDENTITY CYCLE

Before reading the remainder of the chapter, reflect on the following word list. These words indicate ways people perceive themselves. Circle **six** that you think most accurately describe yourself.

beginning	uncertain	student
rebellious	resisting	questioning
loner	free	individualist
cooperative	teacher	directing
scared	tentative	helpless
challenging	searching	testing
unique	separate	detached
nurturing	assisting	reliable

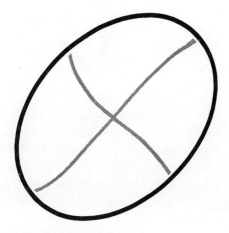

THE FOUR PHASES OF INDIVIDUAL DEVELOPMENT

Just as the Family Map serves as a guide to the varities of family experience, the Identity Cycle describes the pattern of individual development. There are four phases in this developmental pattern: dependence, counter-dependence, independence and interdependence. Taken together they form a cycle which repeats many times in each person's life. The Identity Cycle repeats again and again because each person is constantly defining and redefining his/her identity, continually rediscovering who s/he is. Let's begin by looking at the first phase in the cycle, dependence.

DEPENDENCE

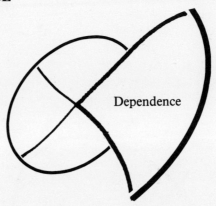

Dependence is most noticeable when children are small. During this stage they need intensive nurturing, attention and affection. Sometimes even as adults we experience circumstances that are overwhelming or too "big" for us. At times like these we wish we could crawl onto someone's lap and be held. An adult has to seek out such nurturance only occasionally. For a child, however, the need for support is constant and vital for natural growth. There is a wealth of accumulated evidence indicating that inadequate nurturing not only affects emotional growth but can inhibit physical growth as well.

At the same time parents are providing support, they need to supply a high degree of structure as well. Children need routines, regularity, rules and boundaries. It is important for them to realize that they cannot do all they want. They need limits which not only protect them from harm but serve as the nucleus of a developing value system. Meeting parental standards becomes one basis upon which children measure self-worth.

Meeting dependency needs for children and adults is central to the development of a self-concept. Support and affirmation from others means that one is important. Care which fulfills dependency needs may supply structure, limits and even decisions. Such care may also extend to doing tasks which the dependent person could do for him/herself. By depending on others the individual can conclude s/he is worthwhile and valued. Since being dependent is a difficult position, however, we soon strive to be independent. First, however, we have to go through another difficult stage called counter-dependence.

COUNTER-DEPENDENCE

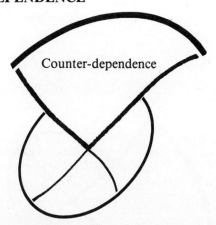

Counter-dependence starts when a child is first able to articulate "no" to his/her parent. It is often budding by the late elementary grades and is in full bloom by adolescence. It is a time when parental judgment and authority are severely challenged in the interest of "making my own decisions." Young persons are exaggerating their need to no longer be dependent which, unfortunately, they still are.

When children are counter-dependent, parents often feel misunderstood, unappreciated, rejected and accused. It is as if to be an adult is to be unjust. In the midst of the struggle parents lose sight of the young person's need for the struggle. Parents worry about whether they are doing the right thing and may feel the child is working against them.

Similarly, the young are lost in all the storm and stress of being an adolescent. They receive support and direction from a new source, the peer group. Suddenly priorities with friends become more important than priorities at home. Not only does time at home diminish, but emotional investment appears to be limited. Counter-dependence is a necessary exaggerated extreme which is vital for a healthy emerging self-concept.

Like dependence, the need for support and affirmation from others continues during counter-dependence. In conjunction with emerging efforts at self-expression, the counter-dependent wants assurance of his/her self-worth. The testing of limits and structure is a way of assessing one's own capacity for judgment and self-direction. When mistakes are made, limits exceeded, or challenges are expressed, the counter-dependent person still needs to know if s/he is acceptable. This is true for both children and adults.

INDEPENDENCE

Independence is a time for establishing autonomy and identity. Whether it is by college, the military or simply a job, the young person must learn how to be self-reliant away from the family. If s/he is fortunate, s/he will have the opportunity to live alone and not in a barracks or dorm. S/he needs to learn how to like being with and responsible for him/herself.

A vital step in any person's growth is learning how to be alone, or separate, as part of learning about relationships. Many primitive societies have elaborate rites of passage which require this experience. The goal is to develop a capacity to affirm oneself from within and to rely on oneself. Independence emerges when approval and support from others is appreciated but not necessary. The ability to enjoy different aspects of oneself is coupled with a realistic knowledge of personal limits and liabilities.

During the independence phase, self-directed energy can be focused on personal projects. Marks of success create a sense of personal competence and self-worth ("I did it on my own"). Personal experiences generate secure and realistic good feelings about self. This step is vital to be able to move into the next phase in the cycle, interdependence with others.

INTERDEPENDENCE

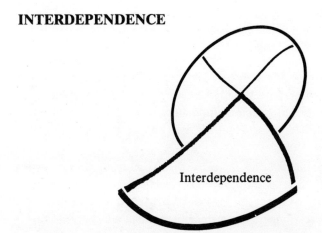

Interdependence is the capacity to appreciate your own uniqueness while being fully involved with others. It requires an established sense of self, the result of successful experiences with independence. It is a phase in which dependency needs do not diminish how a person feels about oneself. In stressful times, a person can lean on others remaining confident that his/her personal identity will not be lost. In fact, an assured sense of identity allows a broadened capacity to see other points of view.

Differences are not so threatening. Responsibility for personal behavior evolves naturally.

With equals, such as in marriage, each person must stake out a sphere, a territory or a role in which s/he can be strong and independent. This becomes a support base from which to establish intimacy, acceptance and self-esteem. It should transcend career, friends and children. To make a place for each person in the marriage is key to its interdependence.

Another characteristic of interdependence is care giving. The interdependent person can teach, nurture and be relied upon without fear of losing anything. It is the mutually sustaining quality that characterizes the relationships of people who have come to terms with themselves, carved out an "emotional place" or identity for themselves, and feel comfortable and accepting in the companionship and care of the other. They have an increased freedom and flexibility because they are rooted in a network of commitments. They have established a personal core that can be trusted.

For children, whose dependency needs are real and whose identity is not fully defined, living with parents who have achieved a high level of interdependence is essential. The care-giving characteristic fosters self-worth. Parents are secure in their sense of identity and their commitments to one another. They appreciate what it is like to be a kid. They do not have to demand that their children become replicas of themselves. Children can be different, develop their own uniqueness, and ultimately form their own identity.

The interdependent person's capacity to affirm from within fosters collaboration with others without feeling threatened. S/he has a sense of the total picture and of the reciprocity of relationships. Interdependence is a significant development phase since it requires an appreciation of other viewpoints as well as one's own. Above all, it assumes a willingness to identify and accept personal responsibility for one's own part in relationship difficulties and to make amends when harm is done. Helping others, appreciating diversity, and integrating divergent needs further enhances a person's sense of self. Like the other phases of the Identity Cycle, interdependence is an opportunity to grow.

SEARCH FOR IDENTITY

The search for identity is a life-long process for all members of the
family. The Identity Cycle for each member varies in intensity and

rapidity but always has as its focus an unfolding self-image. A constant factor in this process is the integration of past learnings about oneself with new expanded awareness.

There is a basic rhythm to the cycle as well. In dependence one seeks affirmation and direction from others. Counter-dependence is a stage in which one seeks to transform sources of affirmation and direction from external to internal sources. It is characterized by trying new things, testing old limits, and seeking new sources of support. Out of this broadening of experience emerges independence. Independence includes the capacity to affirm from within oneself and to be self-directing. No longer are others needed to support, to guide, or even to approve.

Interdependence maintains that self-determining quality but adds the new dimension of supplying affirmation and direction to others. Secure in a confident sense of self, the interdependent person is able to nurture and to assist others without losing or diminishing those hard-won qualities unique to him/herself. In fact, the challenge becomes a continuing source of growth. The cycle becomes complete since a fully developed core of personal integrity then becomes a source of support, direction and modeling for others.

In any stage in life, a person tends to emphasize one phase, or sometimes two phases, of his/her Identity Cycle. Very young children,

for example, are mainly in a dependence phase although they may express counter-dependent behaviors regularly as well. Teenagers may emphasize counter-dependence, yet, at the same time, exhibit many independent behaviors. Even with an emphasis on one or two phases, however, most children, adolescents, and adults will use behaviors from the other phases as well. Furthermore, as a person moves through his/her Identity Cycle, the major phase s/he is emphasizing will also shift.

Yet, once a person has moved through the Identity Cycle, s/he is not a fully developed person. Rather, as circumstances change—patterns become routine and boring, new opportunities arise, preferences shift—the comfort of stable interdependent relationships decreases. In conjunction with this, a person typically begins a new cycle in his/her life-long search for identity. This search, in fact, is a quest that never ends.

CHILDHOOD AND THE IDENTITY CYCLE

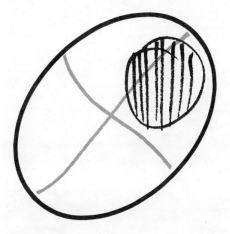

A small child is playing. She climbs into her mother's lap and snuggles. She enjoys the comfort and warmth, yet soon she gets down. Her mother asks her to go pick up her toy bear to which she responds, "No, I don't want to." Mother insists, however, and she puts away her bear with just a touch of disdain for the task. She asks if she can take a bath by herself. Mother agrees. During the bath, the girl gets very upset when Mom checks the water temperature and the girl's ears. The reason is that she wants to do it herself. After the bath, she enjoys sitting in her mom's lap getting her hair dried. She feels her mother's care. When she is finished, she asks if she can help Mom fold clothes. She spends ten minutes helping her mom by folding washcloths and towels. Bored with that she returns to playing.

Within an hour or so, this little girl has experienced all phases of the Identity Cycle: dependence, counter-dependence, independence and interdependence. This experience is common for children. When they seek care, support and structure, ask for help or want attention, they are feeling dependent. Resistance to responsibility and parental demands is counter-dependence. The effort to master something by themselves is a sign of independence. Efforts at cooperation and being together is interdependence. For parents, watching their children grow is like being at a concert. Different instruments predominate during different movements of the same performance. In the chart below are listed a variety of behaviors children use when they are in different phases of the Identity Cycle.

Dependence

Wanting to be cuddled, held and touched. High need for attention. Asking for help in many forms, e.g., picking out clothes, cutting up food, doing school projects. Wanting to be told they are good, loved and competent. Need for limits by parents to prevent dangerous, inappropriate or self-destructive behavior.

Counter-dependence

Ignoring, refusing and challenging requests by parents. Temper tantrums and obnoxious behavior to resist limits set by parents. Concern over what is "fair." Efforts at showing it is other people's fault— especially siblings. Establishment of territories— "the stay on your own side" mentality. Early attempts to run away from home. Comparisons to what other kids get from their parents. Playing one parent against the other. Not wanting to be responsible for tasks or for helping others.

Independence

Playing by self. "Decorating" own room. First trip to store, or hike or bike ride in which child is on own. Efforts to do it "myself." Hobbies, collections, projects, or special skills developed on own which become personal statements about self. Inventing ways to entertain oneself. Creative efforts to "make something up" whether in story, song, or art. Reading the first book by self. Recognition of ways that s/he is different from other kids is first step to self-knowledge.

Interdependence

Learning to play on a team. Efforts to help parents and other family members. Doing special things to nurture and take care of parents; special gifts and recognition of things parents have done. Cooperation in school projects. Taking special responsibilities in school, church, and community. Recognizing when parents and other family members are stressed and trying to assist. Doing what is asked.

Understanding Us; Interpersonal Communication Programs, Inc.

ADOLESCENCE AND THE IDENTITY CYCLE

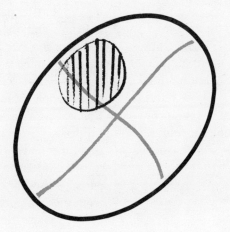

Adolescence seems the most difficult stage in life. The major reason for this is the wide variety of adult skills and behavior that adolescents are attempting to master. Research shows that limit testing and rule bending are part of acquiring new skills. Pilots, for example, go through a stage in which, after having achieved a certain level of confidence, they push the limits of their skills exceeding guidelines prescribed in their training. This predictable phase makes them more dangerous than beginners, who do not have the confidence to try, and veterans, who have the judgment to know better.

Adolescents are experiencing this pattern in many facets of their lives. Because of this, adolescence is often the time when the family experiences the most tension. In the chart below are examples of a number of behaviors adolescents use in each phase of the Identity Cycle.

Dependence

Fear of failure, especially in front of peers. Wanting to be encouraged when starting new ventures and comforted when they don't work out. Need of yardsticks for achievement and success. Help of peers and other adults besides parents becomes increasingly important as models, sources of support and affirmation, and signs of uniqueness. Sensitivity to the opinions of othes extends far beyond family.

Counter-dependence

Chronic challenges and resistance to parental limits. Critical of decisions made by parents and by adults in general. Feelings of being unappreciated—indignant when good works go unnoticed. Oversensitive to slights or statements which can be construed as personal. Efforts to exaggerate differences through dress, language and behavior. Support is sought from peers. Pressure to do things before appropriate or even safe. Threats around impending independent status. Desire to make "own" decisions. Heightened criticism of adult lifestyle, values and hypocrisy. Not wanting to be "saddled" with responsibilities.

Independence

All the firsts, the first driver's license, the first extended trip away from home without family, and the first job. Individual achievements in sports, school, and organizations. Keeping of a diary. Selection of own clothes. Spending solitary time in room. Growing "self-awareness" in terms of values, abilities and limitations. New understanding of personal sexuality. Ability to take care of self with minimal involvement of parents.

Interdependence

Recognizing impact behavior has on other family members and peers. Working on church, school and community projects to help others. Care of younger brothers and sisters. Taking over for parents in special situations. Developing capacity to participate in team efforts or joint projects. First job efforts which require dependability and working with others. Publicly appreciating others for their contribution within family, peers, and other adults. Acknowledging errors and doing something about them.

Understanding Us; Interpersonal Communication Programs, Inc.

Tension is part of developmental change whether for children, adolescents, or adults. Growing children need rules and structure, yet limits are challenged and tested. Any parent who has survived the "terrible twos" and beyond can attest to this. To supply structure for a small child can be a demanding task and an unrewarding energy drain. To struggle with an adolescent who is applying pressure can also feel pretty grim. The child's ongoing quest to establish a separate identity from the parent is coupled with the parent's own fears and, perhaps, feelings of inadequacy about parenting. Trying to cope with children's or teenagers' counter-dependence can be a trying task. Perhaps the only thing more difficult is being a child.

There are several points to recognize which can help parents keep things in perspective. First, **if you believe you are in a struggle, you are.** Challenging parental limits means that a child is right on schedule developmentally. In fact, if there is a lack of challenge as a child matures, then parents should be concerned. Growing up is essentially the process of establishing one's own identity. For a child to not test parental limits may mean impaired development.

Second, **the struggle is not good or bad, it simply is.** When a child is counter-dependent, parents should understand that this does not mean that they are bad or failures or that their child is trying to get them. In fact, misbehavior can be interpreted as an opportunity. No longer is a "good" child one who obeys the rules and a child who fouls up "bad." Rather, a parent can accept that the child is testing limits, which is needed in order to grow.

Be aware, however, of the formidable tactics for resisting parents which young folks have at their disposal. Gerry Patterson, the famous behavior researcher, found that children's methods for avoiding their parents' requests were extremely effective. If a child whines and cries, it will work about thirty-one percent of the time. Even more effective is when a kid foams at the mouth, screams, shouts, and throws a temper tantrum; this is effective thirty-three percent of the time. However, if a child ignores a parent's repeated requests, the parent will eventually give up two-thirds of the time.

For a parent lost in the struggle with children about picking up clothes, keeping a room clean and showing up for dinner on time, it is hard to see that those issues are really not the issue. Notice the parents who have

four children. By the time they get to the fourth, they are much more relaxed about limit setting. They are also clear, on the basis of experience, what needs to be insisted upon. Their experience tells them that **the struggles will pass.**

Dependency issues, however, do not end with parenting. Parents no sooner launch their offspring than they may have to face the prospect of taking care of their own elders whose health may be in the decline. Caring for an older person resurfaces many of the old dependence problems. Struggling to maintain his/her own dignity and respect, an incapacitated senior can be extremely resentful about the caring intrusion of adult off-spring. Insisting that s/he can "do it myself," the senior has the perspective of a life of accomplishment, yet s/he may delude him/herself considerably about the current reality. The situation is ironically parallel to the adolescent.

By maintaining a developmental perspective, an adult can see growth as the interplay of various phases of the cycle. It does not have to be a win/lose contest in which self-worth is at stake. By accepting these phases of identity as a natural part of the growth of children, adolescents or even seniors, they may come to appreciate their own phases of identity as an adult.

ADULTHOOD AND THE IDENTITY CYCLE

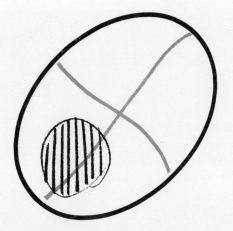

The burst of publications on adult crises and "middlescence" has clearly indicated that the search for identity continues throughout adulthood. The research also indicates that this process in adults is much the same as that of young people growing up. During a discussion in class about the Identity Cycle, one of my middle-aged students observed,

"I've done that twenty-three times!" Like younger folks, adults can be simultaneously in all four phases of the cycle in different spheres of their life.

Adults often become **dependent** when an unusual or unexpected stress occurs. To feel emotionally vulnerable or overwhelmed at the loss of a loved one or a similar catastrophic event is natural and appropriate. Even having a particularly hard day can generate the wish to lean on someone and to feel cared for. If, as a child, you were not nurtured, it may be difficult to seek support. In our culture, men have the hardest time dealing with their dependence feelings because men are supposed to be strong and invulnerable. We have learned that the iron-fisted response to stress results in early death, a high price to pay.

Dependency feelings also occur when starting something new. A new job, or even a new hobby or sport, requires starting at the most basic level, typically with someone to serve as a supervisor or teacher. Usually at this stage we are grateful for assistance and we are anxious when there is no one around to provide it.

Even falling in love can create dependence. Do you remember when you fell in love? The excitement, discovery and caring were so important that you did not want to be apart. Not being able to "exist" without the other, you became preoccupied with the next time you could be together. These moments were a "high" experience and are treasured in our memories.

Counter-dependence for adults is easy to see. In its mild form it may be boredom with the same old routine and mild resentment at unnecessary restrictions. Within a marriage, it might be the frustration at the restrictions of parenthood and marriage which takes the form of judgmental criticism of spouse and kids. In a work setting, it may be the wish for increased responsibility or even to be one's "own boss."

The quest for **independence** is very much an adult search for identity. Creating something on one's own without the help of others is characterized as "making it" or "having arrived." No longer does one need a mentor. In fact, having established a sense of self allows full freedom to support others.

In **interdependence,** the adult recognizes that not only do other people rely on him/her, but s/he must rely on others as well. Not only does s/he provide support and care to others, but s/he receives care and support from others too. The result of this recognition is a profound sense of inter-relationship with spouse, children, relatives and others. Examples of behaviors typical of each phase in the adult Identity Cycle are listed in the chart.

Dependence

Wanting comfort and care during periods of stress and overextension. Asking for help when overwhelmed and vulnerable or when starting new career, project or phase in life. Seeking personal awareness as to competence, attractiveness, and value, and seeking support in critical decisions at significant choice points. Using mentors and models as guides. Feeling immobilized by grief and catastrophe. Desire for someone else to take over for awhile. Taking responsibility for dependency needs with other adults and kids—asking for what they want.

Counter-dependence

Quick identification with the underdog. Supporting causes which are anti-system. Impatient with demands of family life and with nurturing others. Defiance of professional or business practices and rules. Desire to be own "boss" and hypercritical of current supervisors. Demands for private space or separateness. Drastic changes in dress, language and lifestyle. Existential "crises" in which life values are reexamined and challenged. Questioning leads to new models, new methods. Mid-life crises and efforts to recapture youth using young people as models. Resistance to new ways of doing things even when they are obviously superior. Efforts to play the system in order to avoid personal responsibility.

Independence

Spending periods of time alone. Sustained creative effort in craft, hobby, academic, or professional pursuit. Comfort with choice of lifestyle, position, or value that is highly unpopular. Articulating personal space as statement about self. Mastery of set of skills or body of knowledge. The establishment of professional or career status. Fully developed capacity to nurture self; doing nice things for one-self and self-renewal.

Interdependence

Marriage allows freedom to depend on other and support other without loss of self. Parenting involves nurturing and even receiving help which adds to sense of self as well as to awareness of relationships. Capacity to identify harm to others and make amends. Serving as cooperative partner in professional and community life. Able to use system to meet personal needs and objectives of others. Can contribute to the whole without loss of self-direction.

Understanding Us; Interpersonal Communication Programs, Inc.

My father's career path is an example of the complex weavings of adult Identity Cycles. He spent thirty years of his life establishing himself as a well known professional dog trainer. I spent many of my days watching him work with all kinds of dogs—hunting dogs, circus dogs, seeing-eye dogs, security dogs. He loved it and even did local TV and newspaper series about it.

At the age of fifty, he grew restless. He would criticize a career which would demand physical labor the rest of his life. One day my parents announced that he was leaving the dog business. In effect, he was teaching himself electrical engineering and launching a new career. He went on to establish a successful lighting business. At the same time, he carefully coached a younger man into making a success out of the dog business.

The curious part of the story is in its ending. As he approached sixty-five, he became critical of business with all of its stress and time demands. The next thing we knew he was retiring from the world of incandescent fixtures and training a group of young men to take over that business. He started a third career, this time as a trainer of horses. Over and above the obvious elements of counter-dependence, independence, and interdependence, there is the fascinating return to animals.

The reintegration of life themes is central to understanding adult development and identity issues. My father's reaffirmation of his love for animals is a prime example. He rejected that part of himself only to embrace it later. In the interests of making change, our counter-dependence often causes us to reject something in its totality. There is, however, that old aphorism about throwing the baby out with the bath water.

Consider the number of people you have heard complain bitterly about a situation they were in: the military, school, days of financial hardship, a prolonged courtship, or a poor marriage. Yet years later they look back fondly on their experience calling it one of the best or most significant times of their lives. At the moment, however, they could not wait to get out of it. The restrictions imposed by the situation were no longer seen as helpful, and counter-dependence was the solution. In a way, the identity phases are like the path of a pendulum on a clock. Progress depends upon going to extremes and returning to a balance.

Adult development is parallel to the identity experiences of youth. The dynamics present when an adolescent wishes to leave home are the same as when an adult feels s/he has outgrown his/her job. What makes adults different is the necessity to reintegrate their past experiences. Adulthood is characterized by rediscovering old truths about oneself.

SELF-CONCEPT DEVELOPMENT AND THE IDENTITY CYCLE

Individuals grow by having a new experience and then reflecting on it. The reflection is a process of integration and learning. In a family where adults as well as children are growing and learning at the same time, identity issues can become very complex.

What is common for all family members is that processes in the family have a major impact on their self-concept and their self-esteem. Being affirmed by others enables each person to affirm him/herself internally and to affirm others as well. Similarly, being directed by others helps create the ability to be self-directing but also to be a guide for others. The Identity Cycle is an essential process whose basic rhythm is repeated over and over during a lifetime. At all stages of life, the family plays an important role in the process.

Having been affirmed sufficiently to have an internal sense of self-worth, a person can successfully integrate the limits of others with his/her own capacity for determining proper action. If something harmful is done, a person with a healthy self-esteem can recognize that it does not mean s/he is a bad person. Rather s/he made a mistake for which amends can be made.

A person feels unworthy or shameful when there has been inadequate affirmation by others and few successful experiences with meeting standards and limits set by others. The important bridge to being able to affirm him/herself from within was never made. The result is that a person struggling with his/her own feelings of shame and unworthiness has difficulty in deciding proper action. S/he might even have difficulty in asking for help. Because of poor self-esteem, behavior which harms others is seen as indictment against oneself. Accepting responsibility for such behavior is difficult since the inevitable conclusion is that others will abandon him/her.

Because of the capacity to feel affirmed, however, a person with high self-esteem can take responsibility for personal limits and feel sorry if harm has come to others. With low self-worth, a person feels ashamed because of his/her inability to separate self from behavior. Fortunately, since most of us feel shameful at one time or another, the Identity Cycle repeats its rhythm. If we missed affirmation at one point in time, we can receive it the next time around.

Because each family member experiences his/her own Identity Cycle in his/her own rhythm, the family system is rather complicated. The particular structure that develops from the meshing of individual Identity Cycles is more than simply the sum of the parts. Furthermore, the family also impacts on each individual's movement through his/her Identity Cycles. Understanding the relationship between the family and individual members is critical for understanding both. The next chapter focuses on this relationship.

THE FAMILY MAP   Group

INSTRUCTIONS TO PARENTS

Our experience is that couples who carefully discuss the Family Map together and then share their findings with their offspring maximize the program experience. These family conversations promote a more complete appreciation of how families develop. They also foster a much deeper understanding of one another which is the central goal of the program. In your talks as a family, remember that to accept another's viewpoint as reality for them will be to enhance that understanding. The exercise involves two steps:

1. As a couple, follow the directions to complete the Family Map, then discuss results. (Single parents may wish to sit down with a close friend who knows your family well.)
2. As a family, share the results together during Session III or, if you are not enrolled in an UNDERSTANDING US group, share your results with your children during a family meeting as family sharing time.

Family Map Directions

Collect the adaptability and cohesion profiles which you filled out during the first and second sessions of the group. Record each family member's scores in the table at the right.

Take each member's scores and use them as map coordinates. Find the adaptability coordinate by matching the score on the left side of the map. Similarly, match the cohesion score with the appropriate number on the top of the map. Where the two intersect, write the family member's name. Example: If Dad has an adaptability score of fifteen and a cohesion score of twenty, his name would appear in the upper right sector of Region I.

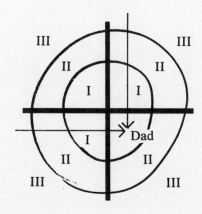

Family Member's Name	Adaptability Score	Cohesion Score

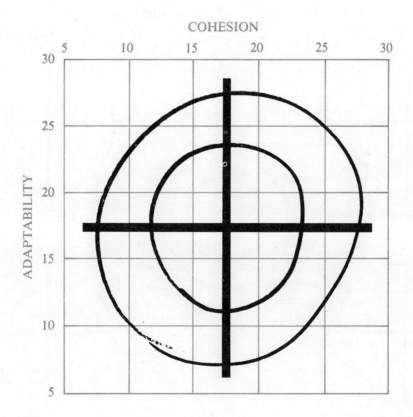

COHESION

ADAPTABILITY

FAMILY MINI-MAPS   Individual/Family

Some families may wish to pinpoint where areas of difficulty are for them. If so, their mini-maps may be useful. Each adaptability scale is matched with a corresponding scale on cohesion. Together they form a score for a mini-map. Each mini-map represents a dimension of wellness which is described in the first part of this section. There are five mini-maps.

Adaptability Scores	Wellness Dimension	Cohesion Scores
Leadership	Collaboration	Closeness
Discipline	Parenting	Support
Negotiation	Problem Solving	Decision Making
Organization	Environment	Commonality
Values	"Us" Concept	Unity

To compute mini-map coordinates, determine each person's ratings for the five dimensions, and write his/her name at the appropriate position in the five mini-maps. The mini-maps can serve as an extra discussion tool for learning more about each other and your family.

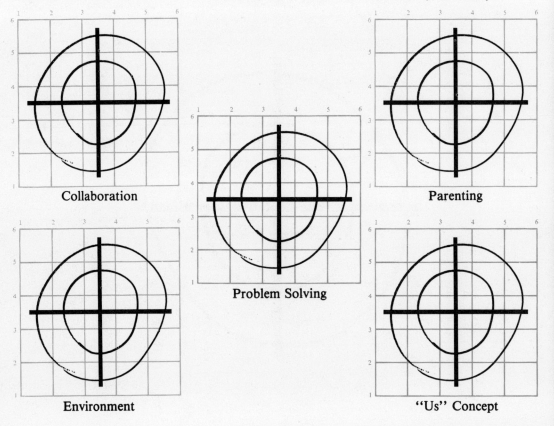

Collaboration

Problem Solving

Parenting

Environment

"Us" Concept

FAMILY-OF-ORIGIN-MAP   **Parent**

Take the family-of-origin totals from the adaptability and cohesion profiles of each spouse, and plot them on the Family Map. Have a discussion about issues that have emerged around the blending of the two traditions. Explore together the ways your respective families were similar and dissimilar.

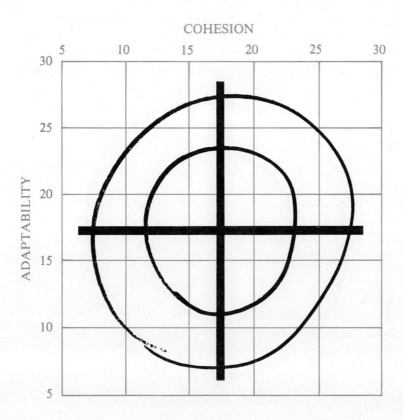

CRISIS FAMILY MAP   Individual/Parent

Using the results of the Crisis Adaptability Profile and the Crisis Cohesion Profile, plot your family crisis score on the Family Map. Once plotted, compare the results with your Family Map and your Family-of-Origin Map. Have a discussion, as a family, speculating about any differences you may notice. Can you think of any specific crisis in which your family operated differently than what appears on the Map?

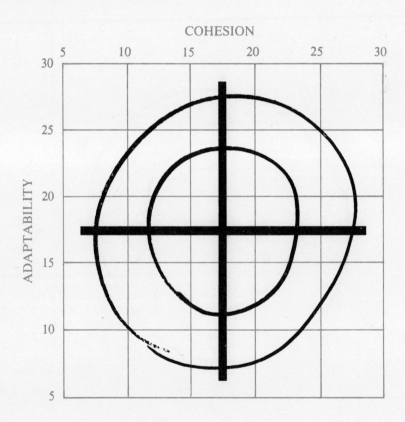

FAMILY OF ORIGIN MINI-MAPS   Parent

Plot the scores of your family-of-origin mini-maps. Note if significant differences occur in any of the dimensions. Include these results in your discussion on your families of origin.

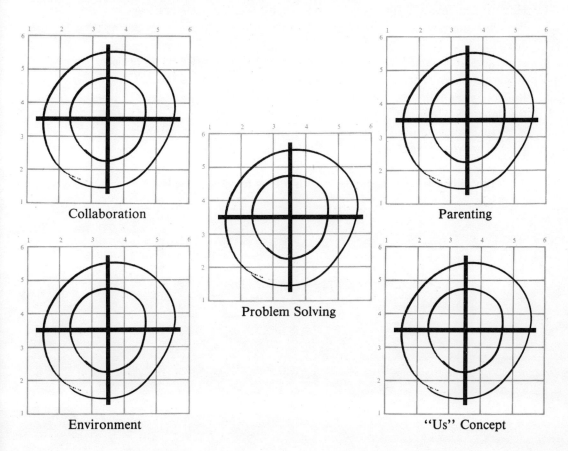

Collaboration

Problem Solving

Parenting

Environment

"Us" Concept

FAMILY JOURNAL ENTRY NUMBER THREE   Individual

This entry focuses on the growth of your family and on your own personal development. As in earlier entries, you are invited to share your reactions to the following questions.

1. How is your family different now from what it was like four years ago?
2. What is your guess about the changes that will occur in your family during the next three years?
3. How does your family compare with the respective family of origin of each parent?
4. What have been some of the biggest changes your family has faced?
5. Reflect on the following four situations. Can you remember any time in your life that fits the description?
   a. A time when you felt vulnerable and helpless, and you needed help.
   b. A time when you challenged the "rules" or the "system."
   c. A time when you were truly on your own.
   d. A time when you worked closely with others to meet a challenge.

IDENTITY CYCLE PATTERNS   Individual

Earlier you were asked to select six words which most aptly described you. The same words are arranged below in terms of dependence, counter-dependence, independence and interdependence. Circle the same six words. Note if any category gets three or more words. What sense do you make of the words that you circled?

Dependence	Counter-dependence	Independence	Interdependence
beginning	rebellious	loner	cooperative
scared	challenging	unique	nurturing
uncertain	resisting	free	teacher
tentative	searching	separate	assisting
student	questioning	individualist	directing
helpless	testing	detached	reliable

WHERE I AM IN MY IDENTITY CYCLE   **Individual/Family**

At any stage in a person's life, s/he tends to emphasize one or two phases of the Identity Cycle. In the table below, give a rough estimate of the percent of time you spend in the different phases. Make sure your figures total 100 percent.

Name						
Dependence						
Counter-dependence						
Independence						
Interdependence						
Total						

Those phases with the largest numbers indicate the one or two which are currently emphasized in your life. You might check with other family members to see whether they see you in the same way that you see yourself or whether their perceptions are different.

Your family may wish to discuss each member's Identity Cycle. If you do, make sure that your discussion is made in a spirit of sharing and learning, not of accusing and labelling. When you talk about your own or other's Identity Cycle, give specific examples to illustrate how an identity phase is expressed by the person you are discussing.

ISSUES AND IDENTITY   Individual

Use the Identity Cycle to explore a current issue in your life. Select an issue which is personal and does not require the help of other people to resolve. Examples would be procrastination, fear of public speaking or time management. An example for procrastination is shown below.

Example:

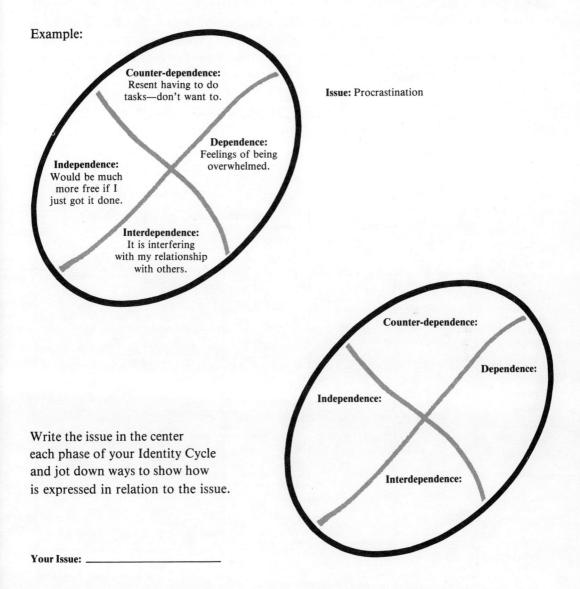

Counter-dependence:
Resent having to do
tasks—don't want to.

Issue: Procrastination

Dependence:
Feelings of being
overwhelmed.

Independence:
Would be much
more free if I
just got it done.

Interdependence:
It is interfering
with my relationship
with others.

Counter-dependence:

Dependence:

Independence:

Interdependence:

Write the issue in the center
each phase of your Identity Cycle
and jot down ways to show how
is expressed in relation to the issue.

Your Issue: _____

IDENTITY AND DECISION MAKING   **Individual**

The search for identity is most intense when facing fundamental turning points in one's life. The following exercise is to assist in reflecting on the connection between key decisions and events in your life and the development of your own Identity Cycle. Fill in the year of your birth and the current year. Select five or six of the most important decision points in your life and mark where they would fall on the time line relative to your own age. Write a brief description of the event. In the columns, record any descriptive words or phrases which may have been accurate about you in each phase of the Identity Cycle at that time. The goal is to locate any patterns which may be typical of you as you confront major choices.

Time Line	Decision	Dependence	Counter-dependence	Independence	Interdependence
EXAMPLE:	Deciding to move away from home at age 18, even though this would be difficult financially.	Fearing that it was wrong decision. Fearing that s/he can't manage on own.	Wanting to be free from parental supervision Critical of family values and practices.	Excited at being on one's own. Pride in having own apartment.	Eager to share holidays with family. Willing to have younger siblings stay stay overnight.
Year of birth					
Current Year					

CHANGING

CHAPTER FOUR

CHANGING

Consider a family of four, mother, father, teenage daughter, and seven-year-old son. For simplicity, let us freeze them for a given instant. The time is late in the day. Dad just arrived home from work preoccupied with a report due the next morning. He is totally absorbed and enthusiastic since be believes that, by returning to work tonight and putting in extra time on the report, he will make a major break-through on his current project. Mom, too, is rushed. She is working on a Master's degree in Urban Planning and tonight her seminar is meeting. The teenage daughter is a gymnast and is anxious to be at a special practice called by the coach that day.

Common to all three of these family members is that each is into his/her own independent interest. Also common to each is the assumption that someone else will be free to watch Billy, the seven-year-old son. He is, at this point, the proverbial fly in the ointment. Billy has had a hard day at school and wants reassurance, attention, and nurturing.

As people rush to get dinner ready, Billy does little disruptive things. He lets the dog in with dirty feet. He demands to be able to feed the cat but spills the cat food. The dog reacts to this by running across the kitchen with dirty feet again. Older family members regard Billy as a burden and a pest. All Billy really wants is to be held and have some attention.

Over dinner comes the discovery that no one really has time to take
care of Billy. In the ensuing debate over who has the most important
priority, Billy begins to feel sad that he is a burden. He begins to feel
ashamed of himself and not worth-while. If this were not just an instant
out of the family's life, but rather an on-going pattern, Billy could have
problems with his self-image as he grows older. It would be even worse if
the family saw his disruptiveness as his problem and did not see their role
in it. The point of the story is that in a family, nothing happens in isolation. Everyone has a part.

This instant in the life of Billy's family is only one set out of all the
possible combinations a family of four could have. Since each person has
four Identity-Cycle options (dependence, counter-dependence, independence, and inter-dependence), there are hundreds of possible combinations within a family of four. Knowing that people can shift their
identity phases momentarily helps one to understand how hard it is to
keep track of what happens in the family.

Some combinations have built-in tensions. Billy's mother, father and
sister had important and legitimate priorities. They simply did not match
well with Billy's dependency needs which were also important and understandable. So the question is how adaptable family members can be in
finding a solution that is acceptable. Family tensions are not the result of
one person creating a problem but rather of the family's inflexibility
toward individual members' needs. To continue to blame Billy would
have perpetuated the problem and not resolved the tension.

Establishing fault is a solution used in all families at one time or another. Some families end up repeating blaming behavior patterns over and over. They have the same hassles over the same issues. It is like a series of instant replays on TV. As we saw earlier, however, families have many options. The four phases of identity provide an essential perspective.

I am always struck by the number of parents who come to the Family Renewal Center with serious problems in parenting. They are unable to set limits, nurture or be respectful. Yet, in structured exercises, they spend extended periods of time with other people's children and display excellent parenting skills. They discover it is easier with other people's children. Their perspective has changed. They find that different options are possible than just the self-defeating patterns they participate in with their own kids. They develop a new perspective and realize that they themselves can do things differently to alter the pattern instead of simply demanding that their children change.

One key to parental perspective is a couple's own sense of interdependence. Interdependency is characterized by a capacity to perceive the whole picture. The problem with counter-dependent and independent extremes is that we tend to have a blurred picture of our own role and a magnified vision of others. A sense of interdependence avoids blaming others for why things are. Rather it seeks to understand how things happened in an effort to change. A person is aware of his/her own part and its impact on others. In a family whose members are growing through a complex interplay of identity phases, an interdependent perspective is vital. If parents lack a well developed sense of self, it will be very difficult for their offspring to develop positive self-images.

There are some risks. I remember one night years ago when my daughter, Stefanie, forced me to wrestle with some fundamental issues about myself. At that time I was a single parent living with two children. I had learned that I could do it; and, in fact, I took pride in my independence. The learnings I had accumulated in my struggle were to serve me well in years to come.

One night, however, I heard Stefanie crying softly into her pillow. I went in and sat next to her. As I held her, the tears subsided. I asked, "How come you're so sad?" She responded, "Daddy, there is no one in this house like me. You and David are alike, but there isn't anyone I can be like." The first overwhelming realization was how much my daughter wanted an adult woman in her life. The second was that, despite my fierce independence, I too missed the company of a woman with whom to share my life. Steffy and I both were sad that night. My commitment to Steffy helped me to accept that I wanted to be married again.

It is my conviction that most adults would postpone many fundamental decisions were it not for their families. Living in a family with an
interdependent perspective continues the growth process for adults as
well as kids. The phases of the Identity Cycle are one way of appreciating
that growth process. The critical relationship is between the individual
family member's search for identity and the family's collective growth
pattern.

FAMILY AND IDENTITY

How a family responds to the identity phases of each of its members is
critical for the development of a healthy sense of self in each person. The
family is a primary agent in the individual's struggle for self-affirmation.
The more unbalanced the match between the family and the individual,
the more difficult the struggle.

It is helpful to see the relationship between family environment and the
Identity Cycle as an equation:

$$adaptability + cohesion = identity$$

The limits provided by the structure of the family combined with the support received in the family are prime ingredients of each family member's
self-concept. Because the different phases of the Identity Cycle involve
differing needs, however, they also require differing family structures to

maintain a balanced equation. Each phase has an optimum family environment which can be found on the Family Map. Dependence needs are most likely to be met in a relatively structured/connected family:

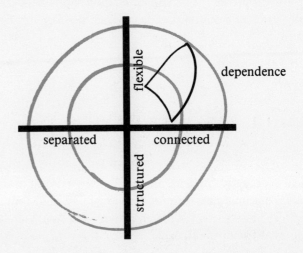

Counter-dependence requires a more flexible environment, yet one that remains relatively connected:

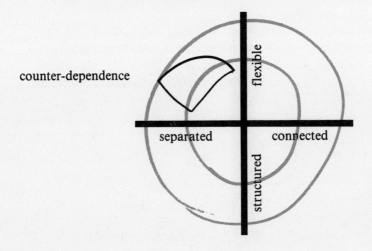

Independence thrives best in a more flexible and a more separated environment:

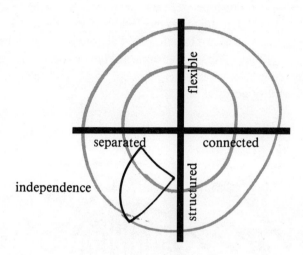

Interdependence works well in all environmental conditions:

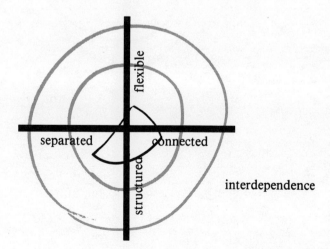

As we saw before, no person is ever exclusively in one phase. Rather, there is usually a pattern of emphasis at a given point in time. An adolescent, for example, may go through periods of heightened counter-dependence. This emphasis does not prevent him/her from also experiencing other phases such as dependence or independence. But s/he more frequently acts in counter-dependent ways. Given the counter-dependence focus, however, there is a combination of adaptability and cohesion which forms an optimum family environment. This optimum range on the Family Map allows for an emphasis on counter-dependent needs but includes other identity needs as well.

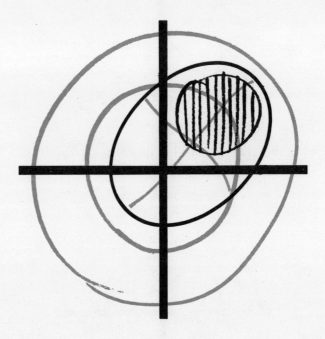

The figure illustrates what might be an optimum range for an adolescent Identity Cycle. It reflects the counter-dependent emphasis on needing more flexibility but maintaining support and acceptance needs. Within this area of the Family Map there is room for some initiatives in totally independent action and also for some dependency needs for structure and support. Interdependent efforts to help in the family can also be met here.

Over time the phases of emphasis within an individual Identity Cycle will change. A small child is dependent upon his/her family for limits as well as emotional support. High structure and high connection are both important at this stage. As s/he matures, the primary emphasis remains on dependence; but a secondary emphasis on counter-dependence emerges, so greater flexibility is necessary. A few efforts at independent action, coupled with the demands of school, start to make their impact; but they still are a secondary emphasis in the Identity Cycle.

With adolescence, however, counter-dependence becomes the focus. The secondary focus is on independent action. As that independence becomes solidified as a young adult, there is a greater recognition of the importance of creating new interdependent structures separate from the family. This searching usually results in life-long commitments which may bring new children into the world. This interdependent commitment fosters the high structure and connection necessary for nurturing small children. The cycle is then repeated. The figure diagrams the progression of the Identity Cycle and the different family environments needed to support each phase in the life cycle.

Obviously every person and every family will experience the process differently. While any of us is capable of any phase of the Identity Cycle, there is usually one or two that are emphasized. This focus determines the best combination of adaptability and cohesion for each person. In the process of developing a family environment to satisfy various members' identity needs, however, families begin to experience tension, conflict, and pressure for change.

IDENTITY AND FAMILY ENVIRONMENT

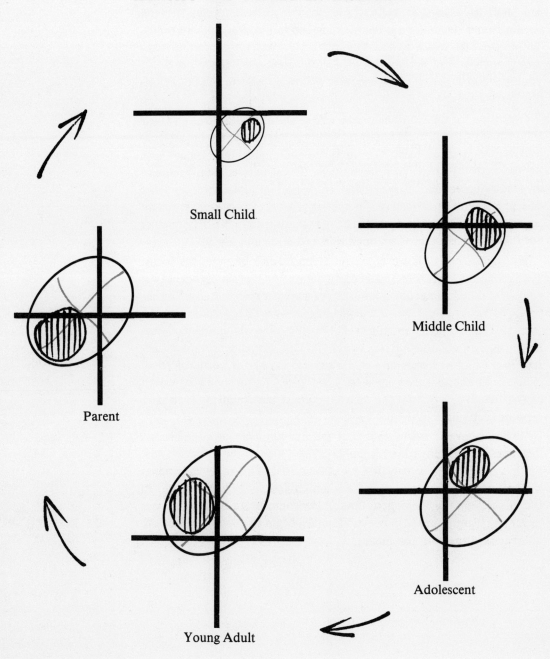

Small Child

Middle Child

Parent

Adolescent

Young Adult

IDENTITY CYCLES AND THE FAMILY COMFORT ZONE

By plotting various family members' Identity Cycles on the Family Map, it quickly becomes clear why families are so complicated. It also becomes clear why few problems occur in isolation. They usually are the result of everybody's involvement.

As an example, we will use the situation of Billy and his family described earlier. The primary emphasis of Billy's Identity Cycle was dependence. The optimum range for him probably would have been in the structured/connected area of the Family Map.

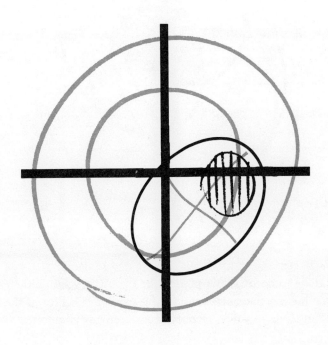

Billy's Mom, Dad and Sister, however, would have been in the more flexible part of the Map:

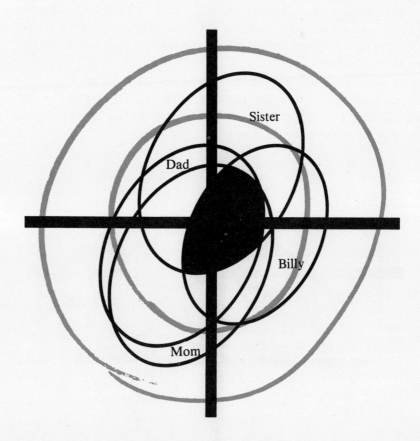

The first thing to notice about placing the Identity Cycles on the Family Map is that there are areas of considerable overlap. This forms the family's Comfort Zone in which identity needs are truly compatible for all.

The tension which occurred in Billy's family arose because, at that moment, various family members needed family environments which did not overlap with those of others. Billy felt extremely dependent, and his Mom, Dad, and Sister were into independent modes of action, as shown in the figure:

Clearly, even in the most healthy of families, there will be moments of mismatch. Note, however, that in Billy's family any of the members could have shifted phases to achieve a new balance. That's because there are enough areas of overlap to create a relatively large Family Comfort Zone.

Not all families have a Comfort Zone. As we noted before, a family of four may have hundreds of combinations of Identity-Cycle patterns, and larger families have combinations numbering into the thousands. With this many options from which to choose, many families have a tough time establishing a balanced system with a solid Family Comfort Zone. It is when the family becomes unbalanced in terms of members' needs that there is family stress.

UNBALANCED FAMILY SYSTEMS

In unbalanced systems, the Comfort Zone is not established or maintained in a manner which fosters the growth of the individual. Either individuals or the family as a whole can contribute to the lack of balance. To ignore individual needs can actually accentuate the issues involved. A child whose dependency needs are manifested as helplessness may at first be ignored by a busy family. The result may be that the child simply becomes even more unable to do things for himself until s/he receives some attention. Similarly, an adolescent's counter-dependent bending of the family rules might be greeted by parents with more stringent rules. The response might be even greater limit breaking.

In both cases the family responded to individual needs in an effort to keep things the same, when really a shift was required. The result was to create further imbalance within the family. Continued to an extreme, this is how blame and scapegoating occur in families. "If only he would straighten up" may be the cry of other family members, not realizing the significance of their parts in the problem.

Some families have great difficulty in maintaining a Comfort Zone for themselves. Examples are single-parent families, families with small children in which both parents work, and families with both toddlers and adolescents. For these families, the nature of the Comfort Zone is especially significant. They have a greater need to shift in and out of different phases in their Family Map because of the special demands of their family's blend of Identity Cycles.

The most unbalanced situations occur in families where no Comfort Zone is fostered and all phases of the Identity Cycle are in some way limited. The resulting extremes of adaptability and cohesion are the outer edges of Region III of the Family Map (Chaotic, Rigid, Enmeshed, Disconnected). Each presents different difficulties in the search for identity.

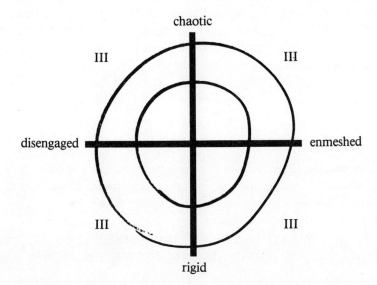

CHAOTIC

To be dependent in a chaotic family is difficult since people are not dependable. The result may be distrust that others can be relied upon. Furthermore, since there is neither a consistent structure to struggle against nor guidelines for measuring success, counter-dependent efforts at self-definition have only limited success. Independent efforts at self-direction can be fulfilling, but they are difficult to sustain because of the unstable support of the family. Finally, interdependent cooperative ventures are seldom successful.

RIGID

The risks are different in a rigid family. Dependence can be prolonged because someone is always available to pick up the slack. This may inhibit efforts to become responsible for oneself. Counter-dependent initiatives are stifled which limits learning about working within structures, especially if performance standards are extremely high. Independent action may be perceived as undermining and rebellious in the rigid family. Tightly specified proscription can limit the amount of interdependent collaboration. An environment in which you do what you are told stifles individual search for identity in the interest of family stability.

ENMESHED

Heightened dependency needs are characteristic of an enmeshed family. Each member sees the other members as, somehow, a reflection or extension of him/herself. Any action is scrutinized to see "what it means about me." Such over-involvement also invites an exaggerated sense of counter-dependence as family members try to untangle themselves from the family web. Like flypaper, however, the more one struggles, the

more involved one becomes. Independence is highly threatening, and separateness may even be punished. The ties among family members are so tight that interdependent cooperation is restricted by individual members' fears of being left out. Sometimes there is even a "family fear" that there will not be enough love/money/food to go around.

DISENGAGED

The sense of isolation which pervades this family does not provide the basic personal affirmation that is key to healthy dependence. Furthermore, the lack of intimacy makes counter-dependence difficult since the essential support during the struggle is missing. Independence is empty since the capacity for self-affirmation cannot be developed. There is also a distrust of reciprocity rooted in the feeling that one has to do things alone. Like being afloat in space, the family member develops a keen inner awareness; but this awareness is rendered meaningless because there is no human contact. There is no one with whom to share, compare, or even struggle and fight.

CONSEQUENCES OF IMBALANCE

Sometimes families mistake what is familiar for their Comfort Zone. Keeping things the same, or not rocking the boat, is at least known, while shifting to something else is new and unknown. Extreme families may not like where they are, but they are used to being that way. Unfortunately, the impact of preserving the status quo may be harmful. It can

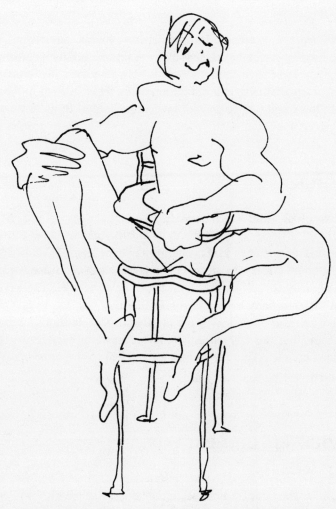

keep a family member in a phase of his/her Identity Cycle inappropriate
for his/her age, or it may drive a family member to an extreme in his/her
current phase in the cycle.

While the extremes present different difficulties for the Identity Cycles
of family members, they generate a common result. Family members are
left with a sense of low self-worth. The fundamental process of being affirmed from without, so one can affirm from within and affirm others as
well, has been disrupted. The unworthiness a person feels will persist until s/he participates in a system making possible the spontaneous generation of a new Identity Cycle.

As we have seen, there are few "pure families" in any category. Rather, families can be at different points on the Family Map, depending on what aspect of their lives together is being considered. The point remains that whether in the middle region of the Map, such as in the example of Billy's family, or in the more extreme regions, the family's capacity for structure (adaptability) and support (cohesion) must strike a critical balance in the face of inevitable change. Each family member depends upon it.

THE FAMILY LIFE CYCLE— STABILITY AND CHANGE

The capacity to shift in and out of its Comfort Zone, or even to change the Zone itself, is fundamental for understanding the family as a changing, dynamic system, yet one which also has a high degree of stability. The strength of a family depends upon the ability of family members to accommodate the changes necessary in their growing together while preserving their essential integrity as a family.

The biggest force for change in a family results from the difficulty of fitting family members' Identity Cycles together. This can create tension,

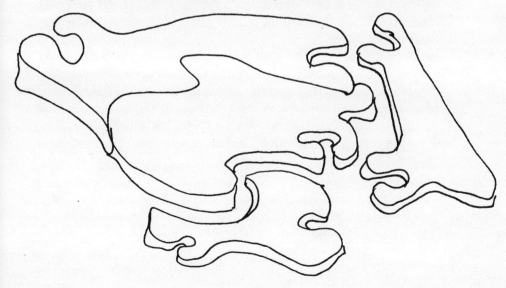

conflict and pressure to change within the family. How well family members respond to the constellation of each other's Identity Cycles is crucial to their satisfaction and growth as a family.

Besides the internal pressures, however, there are external forces for change, too, ranging from shifting economics and cultural patterns to major technological breakthroughs. Similarly, there are forces for stability. Internally, examples are the traditions, values, rituals and models that have been handed down generationally. Outside the family, examples are customary practice and religious and legal sanctions.

Like any human system, the family system needs to be able to change in order to effectively adapt to the changing needs of family members and to change in society. The family also needs to maintain its structure for the security and well-being of its members. A balance is needed which allows for change yet preserves the integrity of the family. Fortunately, members of the family have a variety of options within their collective Identity Cycles to respond to change within the family while maintaining essential stability as well.

FAMILY GROWTH PATTERNS

One of the most significant forces for creating change, yet preserving needed stability, is the maturing process within the family's developmental cycle. In Scene A, small children are dependent and in need of guidance and support from their parents. In Scene B, the children have matured into adolescence and are reaching out for new experiences. The connection between the parents and their teenagers becomes more tenuous requiring trust on both sides. In Scene C, there is independence for the young adults. Scene D reflects further growth into inter-dependence as grown children initiate new relationships and have children themselves.

From an adult perspective, these four scenes carry an added dimension of personal growth and change. In Scene A, young adult parents, who have recently emphasized the independence phase of their Identity Cycles, must adopt a primarily interdependent orientation to supply the structure and support needed by the children. In Scene B, the interdependence is maintained. If they are typical adults, however, they may be experiencing some counter-dependence towards their children in the form of feeling tied down and exasperated with constant limit testing.

Scene C portrays a new-found independence for the parents although they maintain their interdependence as a couple. Scene D contains many possibilities. These are the interdependence towards others, the new opportunities of interdependent nurturing of grandchildren and even of

new sons and daughters-in-law. There is the independence of retirement but also the specter of dependence problems that sometimes accompany advancing age.

The adult maturing process begins with the major change from the independence phase in young adulthood to interdependence as the new family begins to be established. It continues through the Identity Cycle as adults experience stages in their own growth prompted by middlescence, career changes, empty-nest syndrome, and the death of one's own parents. Throughout this process change for adults can place high stress on the family system. Wives who return to work outside the family, for example, may find ambivalence or even resistance on the part of children and husband. To see children as the only persons growing is to miss an important element of life.

The driving force behind changes in the family structure is the movement of all family members through their Identity Cycles. As a child moves, for example, from an emphasis on dependence to counter-dependence, s/he creates unbalance for the family because its structure no longer supports his/her identity needs. This unbalance creates a tension, which may break out into family conflict, as the family tries to bring the child back into line to keep the family in its comfort zone. In turn, the child struggles to change the family so s/he can satisfy his/her identity needs. The child tests limits, challenges parents and other family members, and generally creates difficulties for others.

A typical result of the struggle is that the family shifts its position from Region I of the Family Map to Region II. This is despite the fact that parents are trying to keep the family structure the same! But in doing so, they tend to intensify the current pattern, for example, by increasing the number of rules to create more structure. Thus, in responding to the struggle, parents push the family toward the extreme, and the family ends up in Region II with various issues to handle.

Pressure to move a family out of its Comfort Zone is usually met by resistance from various family members. If a child or adolescent is applying the pressure, parents usually justify their attempts to maintain the present structure by insisting that the child is not "old enough" to do what s/he wants. Actually, of course, the underlying reason is that the familiar comfortable balance of the family system is being threatened.

Although resisting change is natural within a family, the movement out of the Family Comfort Zone is not something to be feared. Rather, it presents an opportunity for the family to readjust itself to better meet family members' needs. What often happens is that, after a period of struggle over the issues which pushed the family into Region II, a new accommodation is reached resulting in a change in the family structure.

Often this change shifts the family back into Region I of the Family Map. Then a new period of balance sets in, with a new Family Comfort Zone, until the next family member moves into a phase of his/her Identity Cycle for which the family structure does not offer effective support. Then the process of tension, conflict and change begins all over again.

When tension and conflict push the family into Region II of the Map, instead of returning to Region I as conflicts are handled, the family may heighten the conflict even further. This may result in a shift of the family to an even more extreme position in Region III of the Family Map. It is a paradox that blocks to change result in change any way, but usually in the opposite direction from what is desired.

The ebb and flow of adaptability and cohesion are a direct result of the identity options each member selects. It is a family environment which sustains the people in the family and, in turn, in which individual choices determine the growth of the environment. In the family there are seasons and cycles which renew. That element of change is critical to growth. When change is blocked, growth becomes limited and sometimes even ceases.

BLOCKS TO CHANGE

Blocks to change are usually a case of "hardening of the categories." To be convinced there is only one way which works is to limit your options. There is strength in having options. Whether for growth or survival, coming to terms with change in the family is important. A number of blocks can crop up to prevent change, however.

BLOCK NUMBER 1: WHEN EPICS FAIL TO BLEND

The first major block to change can occur at the blending of the two epics. Because of differences from their respective families, some couples fail to negotiate understandings about significant issues, such as religion,

birth control or financial priorities. This adds stress to their relationships.

I grew up in a pre-ecumenical era in which diversity of faith was not
tolerated. I witnessed interdependent efforts by spouses to bring the
other into his/her own faith being met with counter-dependent
resistance. The spiritual chasm between them was accentuated at each
rite of passage (baptism, first communion and marriage of children), not
to mention each Sunday morning. The choice for them appeared to be
between being separated from a loved one and betraying the faith of their
parents. Seeing only those two options prevented the exploration of what
they each wanted for themselves. It seemed easier to pretend it was not
an issue. The result was a huge emptiness in what could have been the incredible bonding of a common spiritual journey.

BLOCK NUMBER 2: WHEN THE SOLUTION IS THE PROBLEM

The single-minded pursuit of a specific solution may limit progress or change. For example, there was the rigid father who, in an effort to make his son responsible, placed incredible demands on him. The more pressure he applied, however, the more irresponsible the son became. The solution, then, becomes the problem.

A wonderful metaphor for understanding this paradoxical quality in interpersonal relationships is the story of the couple who purchased an electric blanket with separate controls. The first night they put it on their

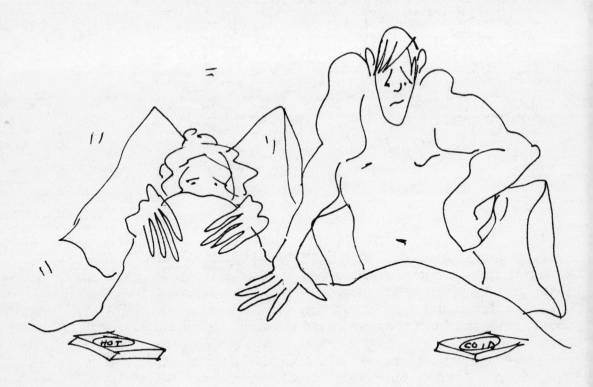

bed, they inadvertently mixed up the controls. He had the switch which controlled her side, and she had his controls. As they went to sleep, she felt cold so she turned up the heat. Since the controls were mixed, however, his side got warm. He felt too warm so he turned his control lower making his wife even colder. She then pushed her control to the top and he responded by turning his off. And so they spent the whole night in misery, neither realizing what had happened.

Couples can spend long, uncomfortable periods with one another and be largely unaware that their own efforts to control the other are producing the opposite of what they wanted. They are aware that things need to change, but they fail to realize that the solutions they are using are at the root of their impasse. By looking to their solutions, they may see that their situation is similar to the couple with the electric blanket. It may simply be a matter of switching controls so that each is responsible for his/her own side.

BLOCK NUMBER 3: FAILING TO ACCEPT RESPONSIBILITY FOR SELF

There are two ways that responsibility for self can become diffused. Both ways can hinder the Identity Cycle as well as family cohesion and adaptability. One way is to be over-responsible and the other is to be under-responsible.

Over-responsibility occurs when you extend your responsibility to include control of others. There are many forms of over-responsibility within the Identity Cycle. In dependence, it is rejecting support and assistance from others when you have need because you believe they cannot handle it. In counter-dependence, it is blaming others for all the problems you have. With independence, it is holding unrealistic expectations for yourself; and with interdependence, it is taking over the duties of others or making decisions for them when they are quite capable of doing so themselves. Most often, over-responsible behavior leads to more rigid and disconnected family environments.

Over-Responsible Behavior

Dependence	Counter-Dependence
Turning away support and assistance when you have need. Not wishing to be a "burden" or an object of "sympathy." Believing others have enough to do without adding your problems. Refusing care because of not wanting to depend on it or owe anything.	Blaming, accusing, and rejecting others as having been wrong about limits and guidelines or inadequate in support. Problems are their fault. Total rejection of others because of their inability to understand. Unwarranted anger and cynicism.
Independence	**Interdependence**
Unrealistic expectations of yourself and others. This is rooted in exaggerated sense of self and diminishes opinion of what others can do. Perfectionism and over-extension limit personal sense of achievement and self-enjoyment. Striving based on comparison to others' performance. To be acceptable one has to be best in all things.	Over-estimation of personal responsibility causes taking over of responsibilities for others. Assumes others cannot do it as well and ends up feeling used. Critical and angry at others for their inability to hold up their end. Denial of personal needs.

Understanding Us; Interpersonal Communication Programs, Inc.

By contrast, under-responsibility for self exemplifies loss of a vital sense of identity. Usually an under-responsible person is unclear about his/her limits or abilities. In dependence a good example is someone who manipulates or cons people into doing something s/he can do for him/herself. In counter-dependence rejection of limits and structure is done indirectly by ignoring others' requests or pretending to have heard them. Independent acts done only for "appearances" indicate a failure to come to terms with oneself. Not asserting oneself in interdependent negotiations may leave a person committed to helping in ways s/he does not want. Under-responsible behavior usually contributes to enmeshed and chaotic family environments.

Under-Responsible Behavior

Dependence	Counter-Dependence
Invite others to take responsibility for things you can do for yourself. Acting helpless and seductive. Seeing things as impossible and hopeless. No one can help me.	Not following through on requests or agreements. Ignoring or even pretending you did not hear guidelines, limits, or requests. When issues occur in relationship, taking them to others but not discussing them with the person.
Independence	**Interdependence**
"Acting as if" one is motivated by personal initiative; however, reality is that personal accomplishments are done for approval by others. Sense of personal inadequacy creates distrust that needs will be met, so must keep up appearances. Genuine self-appreciation fails to emerge. Even when doing well, self-doubt requires external signs of success.	Compliance and acceptance of arrangements which don't fit. Failure to assert oneself in negotiations and commitments. Helping and supporting people when you don't wish to. Becoming intrusive and competitive out of fear of being cut out or ignored. Extremely high inclusion needs.

Understanding Us; Interpersonal Communication Programs, Inc.

Sometimes over-responsible and under-responsible actions go together. For example, take the over-responsible parent who is a sitting target for the under-responsible child. By consistently acting helpless the child is able to avoid being responsible. Taken to an extreme on the Family Map, this could result in a rigid-enmeshed environment.

As an alternative to either over- or under-responsible behavior, each person in a family has the option of behaving self-responsibly. In dependence, for example, this means asking for help when necessary and accepting assistance and care in times of genuine need. In counter-dependence it means being explicit and direct about what you want when testing limits, and it means negotiating issues which emerge from conflicts directly with the people involved. Self-responsible independence means providing direction for yourself, trusting your own judgments and, when you have made a mistake, being able to forgive yourself. In interdependence, self-responsible behavior includes Collaboration with others, accepting responsibility for one's own part while affirming others' contributions, or nurturing, guiding and teaching without taking control over others.

Self-Responsible Behavior

Dependence	Counter-Dependence
Accepting assistance and care in times of genuine need. Adults and adolescents asking for help. Following guidelines and instructions. Seeking of personal affirmation.	Testing of limits and capabilities. Being explicit and direct about what you want or don't want. Recognizing clearly the issues which do emerge and then negotiating issues with person(s) involved.
Independence	**Interdependence**
Developing sense of personal agency and self-direction seen in tasks accomplished by self. Capacity for self-appreciation. Enjoyment of being alone because of who you are, not out of reactions to others. Trust and confidence in personal judgmental ability to survive and to excel. Able to forgive oneself.	Self-assurance allows for easy collaboration and involvement with others. Sharing of life experience seen as further self-exploration as well as opportunity for meeting needs. Taking responsibility for personal part in work and problems while affirming others through nurturing, teaching and guiding.

Understanding Us; Interpersonal Communication Programs, Inc.

Note that a common theme of self-responsibility is maintaining clarity about one's own intentions as well as a realistic sense of personal capacity. To achieve a balance does not mean walking a tightrope between over- and under-responsible behavior. It does mean making a conscious effort to be aware of the broad range of options you have for matching your own needs and limits. This awareness of personal options is vital for family wellness.

FAMILY WELLNESS

Taking responsibility for oneself is the cornerstone of family wellness. In each area of family health (collaboration, parenting, problem solving, environment, and "Us" concept), the role of personal responsibility is essential. In turn, each area of a family's life together contributes an added value to each family member's sense of self. In a family, it is a sign of a healthy:

collaboration when family members pull together to do something, confident that their individual contributions are appreciated and useful;

parenting when children feel successful at meeting parental expectations and supported when they make mistakes;

problem solving when each person takes responsibility for his/her part in a common problem;

environment when care is taken to insure time and experiences together as well as apart;

"Us" concept when people who are together help each one to take pride in who they are separately.

Family wellness consists of keeping as many options open as necessary to maintain environmental balance. For each member this means maximizing the Family Comfort Zone allowed by the overlap of the areas most fitting his/her own Identity Cycles. Awareness of personal options, as well as acceptance of personal responsibility for choosing among them, involves the recognition of two realities.

First is that we all make mistakes and cannot be perfect. By being aware of human possibilities, a person can keep a sense of human limits, recognize that s/he has made a mistake, and simply do it differently next time. It does not mean that his/her relationship with those s/he loves is broken forever. Nor does it mean s/he is diminished somehow as a person by what s/he has done.

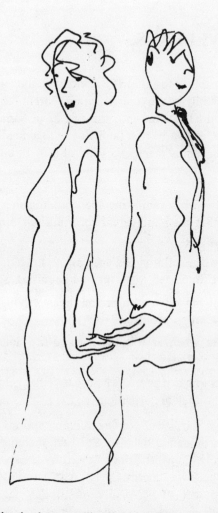

The second reality is that conflict is inevitable, especially with those one loves the most. The basic nature of the Identity Cycle is the very essence of how humans renew themselves. Yet, at its core is a process which requires a pushing away from others even under conditions when everything else matches up. So no family is without pain. To avoid or control the pain simply intensifies it. To acknowledge pain as a sign of growth and accept the inevitable differences paves the way for the reconciliation. The pain then takes on new meaning as the relationship deepens. Differences and distance need not be interpreted as personal failure but as a new period in the family cycle of seasons.

When these two realities are accepted, a confidence in the care of others emerges, coupled with a realistic appreciation of oneself. A mistake may cause pain, but an awareness of options allows that amends can be made. We are all redeemable and can be forgiven.

Key to this is the concept of self-responsibility. Being faithful to oneself is the surest guide to fidelity to others. In an era which has underlined self-realization and independence, we have not noticed that being true to ourselves is also the key to interdependence for, in a family, the fundamental issue is trust. A climate of trust prevails only when you can **depend upon** others.

To maintain trust, two vital processes are necessary. First, when in conflict with others, it is vital to explore fully your own responsibility in the matter. I have often found that the more certain I was that a problem was someone else's fault, the larger my own piece of the action was. Second, it is vital to recognize one's own role in assisting the identity process of others. Self-help groups, such as Alcoholics Anonymous, have known for years that in affirming others a confirmation of one's own identity is realized. Both of these processes—accepting self-responsibility and acknowledging interdependence with others—are at the core of what UNDERSTANDING US is about.

FAMILY RENEWAL

This book and program are about the renewal of families. There have been many excellent books and programs which teach methods and skills. But UNDERSTANDING US tries to tap into the family's own healing process as well. Like other natural systems, families can reassert their own strength as part of an on-going search for their collective self, their "Us," and can continue to draw strength from each member's personal quest for identity. If the resulting family environment nurtures **autonomy** as well as **togetherness,** the inevitable conflicts will be responsively handled and responsibly bridged. Furthermore, the essential elements of a healthy self-concept will be preserved since there is trust for each other. And families will be able to overcome blocks which prevent growth and change.

This concept of family wellness and renewal assumes an almost ruthless realism about ourselves. The honesty necessary has been captured in a prayer useful to many and very much in the spirit of this book:

> God grant me the serenity to
>   accept the things I cannot change
> Courage to change the things I can
>   and wisdom to know the difference.

> Amen.

CONCLUDING JOURNAL ENTRY   **Individual/Family**

The following are some questions to reflect upon in your journal as you conclude UNDER-STANDING US. They are also an invitation to continue reflecting on your learnings from this program. As your understanding deepens, so will the richness of your life as a family.

1. What patterns in myself and in my family do I wish to avoid?
2. In what ways can I keep the sources of renewal alive in our family?
3. What are some steps I can take to be more responsible for myself?
4. Whom in my life do I continue to blame for things I don't like?
5. How can I make sure our family has a regular time to meet, tell stories, talk out issues or plan for the future?
6. What new rituals need to be integrated into our family?
7. What new options am I going to pursue as a result of UNDERSTANDING US?

FAMILY COMFORT ZONE   Family

   Below is a Family Map that can be used to draw a Family Comfort Zone. Each person should draw an oblong which would be the perfect range for his/her own Identity Cycle. Shade in the area where the oblongs overlap—this is your Comfort Zone. Have a discussion about the extent of your Family Comfort Zone. Is it sizeable enough to include all of you at most times, or are some changes necessary? What possible options are there?

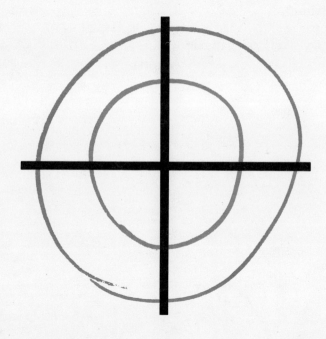

OUR CHANGING FAMILY   **Individual**

Using the Family Map designate three points which indicate where you were five years ago, where you are now, and where you expect to be in five years. For example:

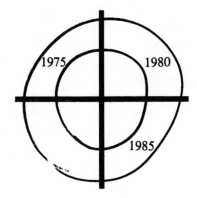

As you plot the dates on the map, have a discussion as a family about what changes have taken place and will need to take place yet. Have a family fantasy about what your life will be like together in five years.

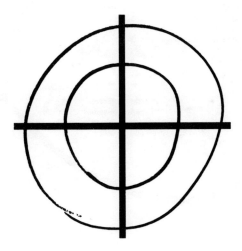

IDENTITY INTERFACE   Couple/Family

A good way to talk about an issue is to share from the different parts of your Identity Cycle. By sharing awareness of the various facets of yourselves, you can gain clarity about the issue as well as affirm one another's efforts to preserve personal boundaries. A more total picture will reduce tension and may even bring resolution. Most of all, looking at the Identity Cycle will help each individual claim ownership in his/her part of the issue.

Consider the story of Dianne and Keith. Keith had been encouraging Dianne to return to school after the birth of their new baby. Dianne took him seriously and enrolled in two courses for the fall semester. When it came down to actually working out the arrangements, Keith became irritable and difficult—especially since one of the courses was in the evening. Dianne became resentful in response to his irritability. When they actually discussed their Identity Cycles, they realized there were many things at stake. The following is how the issue could be diagramed.

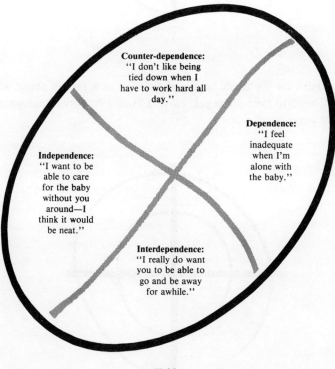

Keith

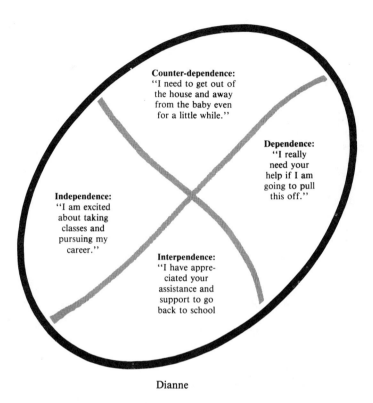

Dianne

By looking at those different parts of themselves, Dianne and Keith were able to clear the air and address some of their respective needs. The Identity Cycle provided a systematic way of talking about the issue.

Select an issue you have with another family member. Use the four phases of the Identity Cycle as a way for each of you to talk through the issue. After some practice, have the entire family talk about an issue in the same manner. It is helpful to use a large sheet of paper and write down each person's reactions, as in the example of Dianne and Keith.

RESPONSIBILITY INVENTORY   Individual

The following questions are designed to help you assess over- and under-responsibility in your Identity Cycle. Complete the inventory by circling the number which most accurately describes what you typically do.

	Never	Seldom	Sometimes	Often	Usually
1. Do you turn away support and assistance when you have need?	1	2	3	4	5
2. Do you blame others about restrictive limits or inadequate support?	1	2	3	4	5
3. Do you believe that to be acceptable as a person you have to be the best in all things?	1	2	3	4	5
4. Do you assume others cannot do tasks as well as you can?	1	2	3	4	5
5. Do you find yourself seeing things as impossible or hopeless?	1	2	3	4	5
6. Do you ignore rules if you don't like them?	1	2	3	4	5
7. Do you try to maintain appearances that you are an independent person?	1	2	3	4	5
8. Do you fail to assert yourself in negotiations and commitments?	1	2	3	4	5
9. Do you not ask for help because you do not wish to be a "burden?"	1	2	3	4	5
10. Do you find rules difficult because those who made them don't understand you?	1	2	3	4	5
11. Do you place unrealistic expectations upon yourself which result in over-extension?	1	2	3	4	5
12. Do you become critical and angry at others for their inability to hold up their end?	1	2	3	4	5
13. Do you like it when others do things for you which you could do for yourself?	1	2	3	4	5
14. Do you "forget" about rules you don't like?	1	2	3	4	5
15. Do you work on personal projects in order to get the approval of others?	1	2	3	4	5
16. Do you help and support others when you don't wish to?	1	2	3	4	5

Responsibility Inventory Profiles

Compute profiles by adding the answers to the questions listed under each phase of the Identity Cycles. Example: If the answers to questions one and nine total seven, circle the number seven after the identity phase. Make a line connecting your answers. Complete both the Over-responsible and Under-responsible Profiles by adding the total scores. Is one significantly different from the other?

Over-responsible Profiles

	Low									High
Dependence (1-9)	1	2	3	4	5	6	7	8	9	10
Counter-Dependence (2-10)	1	2	3	4	5	6	7	8	9	10
Independence (3-11)	1	2	3	4	5	6	7	8	9	10
Interdependence (4-12)	1	2	3	4	5	6	7	8	9	10

Total Over-responsible Score_____

Under-responsible Profiles

	Low									High
Dependence (5-13)	1	2	3	4	5	6	7	8	9	10
Counter-Dependence (6-14)	1	2	3	4	5	6	7	8	9	10
Independence (7-15)	1	2	3	4	5	6	7	8	9	10
Interdependence (8-16)	1	2	3	4	5	6	7	8	9	10

Total Under-responsible Score_____

As an experiment, family members may wish to compare their total scores and their Family Maps to see if over- or under-responsibility in your family is reflected your family environment.

SEARCHING FOR OPTIONS   Individual

Some problems are rooted in our lack of options. The repetition of old solutions does not resolve anything and may even be a part of the problem. The question then becomes one of going beyond the solutions already tried. Use the following questions as a guide in thinking through a persistent problem.

1.   The nature of the problem is...

2.   Solutions I have tried so far are...

3.   New possible solutions are...

4.   One new solution that makes sense is...

5.   One step towards that solution would be...

FAMILY MEETING   Individual/Family

The goal of a family meeting is to have a regular time together to discuss family issues, goals and plans. To be successful, it needs to be regular and useful. Family members need to feel as if their input counts. It is a good way to preserve order and balance, as well as to maximize opportunities and options. It can add to the Family Comfort Zone.

If you do not now regularly meet, call a session in order to plan a trial series of meetings. Pick a time which can regularly be observed. If at first it feels awkward, think of the blocks to change.

THE FAMILY RETREAT   Individual/Family

The Family Retreat is designed as an exercise to foster personal responsibility and appreciation. Each person takes some time to respond to the questions asked in the retreat. The family can then share their responses, taking great care not to tease, put down or be critical of other family members' statements. The process is intended to help you overcome fault finding, accusing and blaming by asking members to accept personal responsibility and to express appreciation. Allow plenty of time when you do this, as it can be a very rich experience.

Divide a sheet of paper down the middle. On one side make a list of what you have done to make it difficult for people in your family to live with you, i.e., things you have done which have been hurtful, demanding or unresponsive. On the other side, list all the things you appreciate about members in the family, i.e., things you truly cherish about others. Then discuss the two lists as a family.

Remember, if someone admits something you have been wanting them to admit, don't do anything critical in response—no joking or put-downs. A respectful and affirming response will provide you with a meaningful, worthwhile time together. This is an excellent family ritual you may wish to institute.

APPENDIX

If you have enjoyed participating in the Understanding Us program and benefitted from the experience, you can qualify to teach the program to other families. Understanding Us Instructor Training Workshops are specifically designed to train you to teach the program. To inquire about UU Instructor Training Workshops in your area, return the Information Request Form in the back of the book.

We also invite you and your spouse or a friend to participate in other ICP programs.

COUPLE COMMUNICATION I

Over 75,000 couples have participated in COUPLE COMMUNICATION which is designed to enrich communication between partners. CC focuses on the processes of flexible and effective interpersonal communication. CC helps partners grow personally as they develop more fulfilling ways of relating to each other while dealing with day-to-day issues. Partners learn frameworks and skills presented in TALKING TOGETHER.

COUPLE COMMUNICATION emphasizes learning-by-doing. Five to seven couples meet with a CC Instructor for four three-hour sessions. Exercises provide practice using specific communication skills with feedback from other participants and the Instructor. Between sessions, partners experiment with the skills and concepts taught in the program and report back to the group on their experience.

PROGRAM TEXT

TALKING TOGETHER presents the frameworks and skills taught in CC. It is clearly written and illustrated with numerous examples plus exercises to help partners learn specific skills and concepts to improve their communication.

Couple Communication was developed by Drs. Sherod Miller, Elam W. Nunnally and Daniel B. Wackman at the University of Minnesota Family Study Center in cooperation with Minneapolis Family and Children's Service. The developers received awards for their research and program development from The National Council on Family Relations and from the Association of Couples for Marriage Enrichment. Over 25 research studies have been conducted on CC. Reports on CC have been printed in THE NEW YORK TIMES, PSYCHOLOGY TODAY and WOMEN'S DAY as well as many professional journals and books.

WORKING TOGETHER

WORKING TOGETHER is designed to help anyone communicate more flexibly and effectively on his/her job. The program enables people to make significant interventions at appropriate times and places on the job in order to help people and projects move ahead. Besides helping to handle tough situations better, participants will learn how to build stronger working relationships which prevent crises from occurring.

WORKING TOGETHER is divided into five modules:

MOD 1. Understanding Yourself helps participants become better processors of the wealth of information inside themselves by using their Awareness Wheel. The Awareness Wheel is used throughout the program to create a practical and uniquely integrated system of concepts and skills. Module 1 includes six basic skills for sending clearer messages.

MOD 2. Understanding Others emphasizes understanding co-workers' awareness. It teaches four specific attentive listening skills and the shared meaning process.

MOD 3. Styles of Communication sensitizes participants to differences in styles of communication and introduces a style which is missing from most people's repertoire—Straight Talk. This style is especially important for dealing with critical issues and situations.

MOD 4. Mapping Issues presents an exciting tool for using self/other awareness and communication skills in decision making, supervision, consultaiton, and conflict resolution.

MOD 5. Building Self/Other-Esteem shows how the attitudes people hold about themselves and their co-workers influence their communication and either build or destroy people and production. This module includes a checklist for discovering why things aren't working, while it also serves as a practical guide for getting things moving again.

The five modules can be taught in a variety of time schedules.

PROGRAM TEXT

WORKING TOGETHER presents the frameworks and skills taught in the program in clear and understandable terms. It contains a variety of exercises to help in transfering of concepts to practical situations on your job.

WORKING TOGETHER was developed by Drs. Sherod Miller, Daniel Wackman, Dallas and Nancy Demmitt in response to requests from many people who participated in the Couple Communication Program for a similar course in business.

FOR MORE INFORMATION...

For the name(s) of a Certified Instructor in your area for any of the ICP Programs mentioned above, or for information on Instructor Training return the Information Request Form.

INFORMATION REQUEST FORM

Please send me the following information (check all that apply):

    Name(s) of Certified ____Understanding Us ____Couple Communication I ____Working Together instructors in my area.

    Information about enrolling in an ____Understanding Us ____Couple Communication I ____Working Together Instructor Training Workshop(s).

Name _____

Address _____

City and State_____Zip_____

Occupation_____

Return to: Interpersonal Communication Programs, Inc.
          300 Clifton Avenue
          Minneapolis, MN 55403

BOOK ORDER

If you would like to order any of the books published by Interpersonal Communication Programs, please fill in the appropriate information below and return this form with payment:

	Price	Quantity	Amount
Couple Communication I: Talking Together	$ 8.95	_____	_____
Alive and Aware	$ 7.95	_____	_____
Making Change	$ 6.95	_____	_____
Making Change Trainer's Manual	$ 5.95	_____	_____
Working Together	$49.95	_____	_____
MN residents add 4% sales tax			_____
TOTAL AMOUNT PAYABLE			_____

Payment must accompany order. Make checks payable to:
INTERPERSONAL COMMUNICATION PROGRAMS